Thomas Richmond

God Dealing with Slavery

God's Instrumentalities in Emancipating the African Slave in America

Thomas Richmond

God Dealing with Slavery
God's Instrumentalities in Emancipating the African Slave in America

ISBN/EAN: 9783743417687

Manufactured in Europe, USA, Canada, Australia, Japa

Cover: Foto ©Lupo / pixelio.de

Manufactured and distributed by brebook publishing software (www.brebook.com)

Thomas Richmond

God Dealing with Slavery

GOD DEALING WITH SLAVERY.

GOD'S INSTRUMENTALITIES
IN EMANCIPATING THE AFRICAN SLAVE
IN AMERICA.

———o———

SPIRIT MESSAGES

FROM

FRANKLIN, LINCOLN, ADAMS, JACKSON, WEBSTER,
PENN, AND OTHERS

TO THE AUTHOR,

THOMAS RICHMOND.

———

"They cried—their cry came up unto God
  by reason of their bondage."
"And God heard their groaning."—MOSES.

"Try the spirits, whether they be of God."—JOHN.

"He that hath ears to hear let him hear."—CHRIST.

"Speak all thy thoughts, O thinker, howsoe'er
They flout the speculations of the age,
Its pet conceits and fantacies."—POLLOCK *Spirit*.

———

CHICAGO:
RELIGIO-PHILOSOPHICAL PUBLISHING
HOUSE
S. S. JONES PROPRIETOR.

———o———

1870.

INTRODUCTION.

No apology is offered for presenting this book to the reading and thinking public. It is ushered into existence by a power and authority above that of the apparent author.

A Divinity that moves and sustains the universe, the Power that projects into being all existence, has produced the materials of this book, and concentrated its elements in the author, with an irresistible force and power, causing its compilation and publication.

The object of this work is to show that God rules and controls the movements of men and nations *now* as manifestly as He did the Jewish nation in olden time. Especially is it given to show that the late civil war in these United States was produced and conducted by Him through His chosen instrumentalities, for the purpose of delivering four million human beings, held as slaves, from cruel and unjust bondage, and also inflict a just retribution for the sin against humanity perpetrated by the American people for more than two hundred years. God moved upon the spirit of the nation, working through the various ramifications of American sentiment, and forms of government, to inaugurate the strife. He then guided it to the removal of the infamous crime of negro slavery. The moral and religious sentiment of the people was not sufficiently elevated and pure to do this work of justice. God had appealed to it many years in vain. He next resorted to the lower passions of the slaveholder, which manifested themselves in rebellion against the national government, and ultimately accomplished the desired object. "The wrath of man praiseth Him."

GOD USES INSTRUMENTS.

A few years preceding this great work, and preparatory to it, God, through that scientific philosopher, Dr. Franklin, and others, "rent the veil" between this material world and the world of spirits, opening the way by which spirits could communicate to mortals, by using their natural faculties.

A NEW DISPENSATION

of life, a new mode of divine manifestations was introduced, a living, active commerce was opened between the spiritual and material worlds, by which the wisdom and sympathy of the upper is transmitted to the lower world, to our conscious material senses.

INTRODUCTION.

A CONGRESS OF SPIRITS

composed of the former statesmen of this country and persons of governmental experience abroad, who felt an interest in human welfare and the rights of man, existed. Dr. Franklin, of Revolutionary days, the early Philadelphia printer, he who first brought electricity under human control, was constituted communicator of the wisdom and plans of that Congress to mortals. The author of this book was appointed by the same authority to receive, impart, and promulgate the wisdom thus communicated by Dr. Franklin to him, through the appointed medium.

Dr. Benjamin Franklin's history is well known by the American people, and needs no comment.

President Lincoln is known throughout America and the world, as the great visible instrument of the emancipation of the African from slavery. His letters to the author since he passed away, as well as the messages from Dr. Franklin and others, prove that he was controlled by the Divine Mind acting through this author's brain; they show that this was the channel of power from the world above, acting upon the national mind.

Dr. Farnsworth, the medium through whose hand the messages were written, is known as a writing medium, answering sealed letters for a time. At the commencement of the war Dr. Franklin perfected his development as a mechanical writing medium, and used him up to the present time.

INTRODUCTION.

Nearly all of the communications in this book were written mechanically through his hand, without pay, by the spirits whose names appear.

Dr. Franklin is the controlling spirit of this work; most of the messages are from him. There are some from John Q. Adams, Wm. Penn, Danl. Webster, J. C. Calhoun, Andrew Jackson, Abraham Lincoln, George Washington, I. T. Hopper, Napoleon Bonaparte, Joan of Arc, Mary, Queen of Scots, Josephine, and others. These messages cover a period of ten years; the subjects were the war, reconstruction of the national government, and the amendments to the Constitution. Notwithstanding their apparent sameness, there are no two messages alike. Each one has a fact, thought, or idea, which no other one contains. The numerous spirits and various dates make up a good variety.

The fact that for ten years the spirits wrote to me on the same theme, the various minds communicating, and the constancy with which they dwelt upon the leading subjects, ought to convince every honest mind of the truth of the grand idea, that God inaugurated the rebellion, and worked out its results through the instrumentalities herein named.

I ask the indulgence of the learned reader for what to him will appear a great lack of good taste and refined language. I have no pretension to literary acquirements. More than fifty years of active business life and correspondence have given me a mode of expression more befitting that life than authorship. This mode of expression I have used in this book — always laying more stress on the facts, truths, and principles given, than the dress in which they are clothed. This is the first book of my production — contains the first thought of being the author of one. This thought came with the request of Dr. Franklin to me, in June, 1866, to gather up the communications that are in this book, compile, and publish them. I offer it to the reader for its *intrinsic worth*, and not for its polish or style. Read it for its truths, its science and philosophy! Read it to cure your infidelity, and to quicken and cultivate your religious nature. Read it for its facts and history. Read it to establish and strengthen your faith in the Wisdom and Power that works this great universe with the precision of perfect mechanism. Read it, though it lacks the polish of literature, or rhetorical order and science :

"Be true, O thinker, to thy nature's law,
"And borrow not another's style, but speak
"Thine own brave thoughts in thine own spirit's tongue.
"Call things by their right names, right minds shall hear."
POLLOCK *Spirit*.

To those who have known me as a business man for years, I need only say that I was acted upon by an irresistible power above me, and gradually developed and drawn into God's service in a work of national justice, as unexpectedly as St. Paul was changed from the work of persecuting Christians, to that of preaching Christ. The same power that called Moses from his sheepcote, called me from commercial pursuits, and for the same purpose—of securing justice to oppressed humanity.

For those who are unacquainted with me, I copy a paper given by my old business friends in Chicago, recommending me to office in the government, under President Grant, which paper never was presented to him, as I felt that I could not confine myself to such a place as I knew that my ability demanded.

Be it understood that this paper relates *solely to my fitness for office under our government, having no reference whatever to this book, or my religious faith.*

I have given an exceedingly brief sketch of my business, religious, and spiritual career. My effort for brevity leaves but a skeleton of what it should be, to present me fully and fairly. This private history was not of my own prompting, or to show myself to the world, but was given by the special direction of Dr. Franklin, as an essential basis of this book. And so I send the book to the world upon its own merits.

CHICAGO, March 1, 1869.

U. S. GRANT, *President :* — We, the undersigned, old inhabitants of the City of Chicago, having been acquainted with Mr. Thomas Richmond for many years, as a resident and an active business man in this city, take pleasure in recommending him to your favorable notice and consideration, for any office that he may desire.

INTRODUCTION.

We regard his business experience, capacity, industry, and integrity, equal to *any position he may ask* in our government. He has been from the first an earnest and consistent Republican, and was a soldier in the war of 1812.

Chas. V. Dyer,
Wm. B. Rogers,
Henry G. Young,
A. J. Averill,
S. W. Stryker,
J. Nottingham,
Saml. T. Atwater,
Howard Priestly,
Egbert Jamison,
J. H. Knowlton,
A. A. Sample,
C. Y. Richmond,
T. W. Steele,
Mahlon D. Ogden,
L. Laflin,
S. Clary,
Thos. Church,
Albert Crosby,
George Keyes,
John T. Lester,
F. Tuttle,
J. C. Walter,
H. Hayes,
A. Duncan,

Matthew Laflin,
Wm. Bross,
Geo. M. Higginson,
O. S. Hough,
F. W. Pratt,
C. Follansbee,
H. W. Blodgett,
Chas. B. Brown,
Thos. H. Marsh,
Frank Scales,
F. M. Kanzler,
Jas. A. Smith,
Chas. Scott,
L. P. Hilliard.
C. Beers,
I. Y. Munn,
Geo. W. Gage,
Jas. VanInwaggen.
Chas. Hinckley,
William Brine,
S. A. Kean,
I. N. Arnold,
C. B. Smith,
German Smith.

INDEX.

	PAGE
My Youth and Minority	9
In the Army of 1812	11
First Journey West—How Employed	12
Now of Age, and Began for Myself	13
First Shipment of Salt—First Credit	15
Spent a Winter Studying Law	18
First Shipment of Salt to the Upper Lakes	19
Purchased Land—Laid Out Village in Ohio	21
Moved to Richmond, Ohio, and Commenced Business	23
Suspension of Banks—Great Embarrassment of 1837	24
Became Member of Ohio Legislature	25
Commenced Business in Cleveland	26
Removed to Chicago	27
Became Member of Illinois Legislature	29
Built the Richmond House, Chicago	30
Built and Sent Vessel to Liverpool	30
Took the Agency of N. Y. C. R.R., and Steamers	32
First Sermon Heard and Remembered	39
Religious Experience	42
Built Large Church in Richmond	46
Member of Presbyterian General Assembly that Tried Albert Barnes for Heresy	47
Left the Church for its Slaveholding Complicity	50
Interview With Spirit of Mrs. Chester	52
Daughter Carrie First Entranced	55
Carrie Passed Away	56
At J. Q. Adams' Request We Hold Circle	56
German Minister Visits Me	60
Passed a Summer in New England	61
Passed a Winter in Boston	62
Took Baths in Salem by Dr. Rush's Orders	66
My Mode of Obtaining Truth	67
J. Q. Adams' Letter	72
Miss Barrett's Visit to Spirit Congress	74
"Circle of Three" Formed	75
Andrew Jackson's First Letter	77
I. T. Hopper's First Letter	78
Letters from Napoleon, Joan of Arc, Josephine, Mary, Queen of Scots	80

INDEX.

	PAGE
Franklin and Adams Call Me to Boston	81
My First Letter to President Lincoln	97
Franklin's Seven Letters on Philosophy of Spirit Control	102
My Letter to Gov. Todd, of Ohio	118
My Second Letter to Lincoln	124
Franklin Tells How He Influences Lincoln	129
Use of "Circle of Three"	129
How Spirits Live	130
My Third Letter to Lincoln	134
Daniel Webster's Letter to Me	137
Wm. Penn's Letter to Me	138
Patrick Henry's Letter to Me	140
Lincoln's (Spirit) First Letter to Me	143
" " Second " " "	145
John Quincy Adams' Letter to Me	146
Franklin's Account of My Development	150
Daniel Webster's Letter to Me	153
Letters from Adams and Franklin	154
Andrew Jackson's Second Letter	156
Josephine's Second Letter	157
Mary, Queen of Scots' Second Letter	158
Letters from Napoleon and Joan of Arc	160
My Letter to President Johnson	161
My Letter to Chas. Sumner, U. S. Senator	163
" " " Thaddeus Stevens	163
My Letter to Franklin and His Reply	164
Arrived at Washington — Note to Franklin	170
Franklin's Reply	170
John C. Calhoun's Letter to Me	175
" " " Communication in Banner of Light	176
Franklin Sends Me to the White House	181
Franklin Wishes Me to Mingle with Congressmen	186–8
Johnson's Trial — Bribery in Senate	189
Franklin Gives Diversity of Mediumship	195
Franklin Directs Me to the Medium at Waterford	196
My Letter to Senator Trumbull	197
Johnson's Impeachment — Senate Vote	199
Franklin's Reason for Change of Visit to Letter	200
I. T. Hopper's Second Letter	201
Franklin Directs Me to Write Gen. Grant	203
How I am Used in This Work	209
Farnsworth, the Medium, Brought to Chicago	213
Franklin's Conditions of Control	214
Lincoln's Third Letter	219
Washington's Letter	220
Franklin Surveys the Past	221
Franklin's Closing Paper	226
The Argument	230

THE AUTHOR'S EARLY HISTORY.

CHAPTER I.

I was born in the town of Barnard, in the state of Vermont, December 8th, 1796. My parents were farmers, and in very moderate circumstances. I was the fifth child and third son in a family of ten. The country was new, mountainous and cold. It required the constant and severe labor of each of the family, from their earliest ability to labor, and the most rigid economy in the whole family to maintain itself, and supply only the *actual needs* of each person.

Appropriate labor was furnished and imposed upon each child, as he became able to do something.

In those early days there was no manufacture of cotton goods, or clothing of any kind, in this country, except what was done in families. Each family of farmers manufactured clothing for itself from flax and fleece raised by themselves. There was no commerce of any amount then and there;

it was all that the people could do to support themselves and improve their farms.

The opportunities for education were very limited, although education was highly appreciated by the inhabitants. The towns were districted, and schools kept, more or less, in each district. In the district I lived in, there was a school kept by a female, three months in summer, and by a male, three months in winter, usually.

Living remote from school, I had a poor chance to attend, but finally, being a good scholar, obtained what was termed a fair common-school education; attending school only when I could be spared from farm work.

As the family grew up, one after another, each in turn, had to go out to work. As our farm did not furnish work for all the family,—nor did it furnish support for it,—we had to dispose of our labor as best we could, to supply home deficiencies.

In those days, people never talked about making money or getting rich, as now-a-days. The only concern then, was how to live,—how to support, educate, and bring up their growing families. People only bought what they could pay for by exchange of commodities, and they paid for what they bought. There was scarcely money enough in the country to pay the taxes. There was a good reason for it. The people raised nothing to sell of much moment,

In my sixteenth year, I was hired out by my father to John Foster, for six months, to work on a farm, at ten dollars per month, for which my father was to have money enough to pay his taxes, and the rest in young cattle—these were called "neat stock." At that age I did a man's work with other men in the field. The next year being 1813, I was in my seventeenth year. I enlisted in the one year's service, in the army. This was in the war with Great Britain, in 1812. Government paid a bounty of sixteen dollars, on enlistment, and eight dollars per month wages, and furnished the following rations: one pound of bread or flour, one pound of beef or fourteen ounces of pork, half a gill of vinegar and a gill of whisky; I think I have this correct. I was selected by an officer to wait on him, so I had no hard military service to perform; indeed, I was in the country with my officer, on recruiting service some three or four months. I saved and returned to my father all my wages drawn from government, and returned home again to work on the farm as formerly.

My mother died when I was in my twelfth year of age. My father soon married again, and had an increase of family, promising to be somewhat numerous.

Home became not as agreeable as I could wish, and I sought of my father my time, to allow me to go from home and get my education. My ambition was to be a lawyer, when I was about sixteen years old. He thought that he would give me my time after a year or two, but the time had never come when he could spare me.

In my nineteenth year, by his advice and consent, I left home for the West, with one Zadoc Thompson, a young friend, both bound for Central New York, intending to take schools, having learned that there was great want of, and high wages paid to teachers.

We started on foot. Each had his clothes tied up in a home-made linen handkerchief, and provisions enough to last a few days. This was in September, 1815.

We traveled, on foot, together, to what was then called Salt Point, being now the first ward of Syracuse. The land where the body of Syracuse now is, was then a cedar swamp, too soft for an animal to pass safely in the summer time.

Here, being offered twenty-five dollars per month to work on a boat on Onondaga Lake and Seneca River, I accepted it, leaving my friend Thompson to go into the country alone. This price for work seemed enormous, having recently worked for ten dollars. It tempted me to abandon the idea of being a school teacher for the present time. I continued to work on the boat until it froze in, and was stopped by ice. I then hired out to tend a salt manufactory. My work was called "boiling salt." The manufactory was called "a block of kettles."

I continued until late in April, the following spring, when I collected my earnings and returned on foot to my father's, the distance being two hundred and forty miles. I walked it in six days. What I earned, I carried to my father. I worked during the summer on my father's farm, and in the fall, I took my wardrobe as before, and went again to Salt Point, on foot, walking all of the way in six days. I worked there again through the winter, returning in the spring with my earnings to my father, and working at home that summer, as formerly. This made four times that I traveled over that road, performing the journey of two-hundred and forty miles in six days each time (except the first), carrying my clothing and a supply of provisions.

This fall, 1817, being 21 years old, and, according to the Puritanic usuage of New England, served out my time fully with my parents, I started as a free man for the West, determined to be a rich man before I died. A neighbor of ours going West with an extra horse, allowed me to ride him, which I thought a great favor. I arrived again at Salt Point, with only a shilling in my pocket, which I kept for more than thirty years as a charm.

Having worked out my minority, I felt right in leaving, although my father urged me hard to remain and take the property, the charge of the family, and support the parents. The young family had become numerous already, with the possibility of further increase. I felt that I had been faithful and just to them, in serving my full minority. Now, I was free to act for myself, and it was my right to leave that old home, and just to myself to pursue my own chosen way. So with the blessings of the family, and their prayers for me, and mutual good wishes and farewells, we parted.

Safely at Salt Point, I felt my new condition: A *free man.* Myself, my labor and my earnings were all my own.

The one great idea of becoming rich inspired me to effort, and to overcome all obstacles. I went to work with a will, and the following winter I tended a salt-block alone,—it being two men's work. My first aim was to acquire three hundred dollars. This would take me to a level with some other young men of the place.

Salt Point was remarkable then for fever and ague, and its severity. My very hard work, and the coming of warm weather, in the spring and early summer, brought on this disease with great virulence. I had, however, accumulated my cherished sum of three hundred dollars.

About this time I received a letter from my father, stating that an old debt, which he had owed from my childhood, was pressing him, and that (if possible) I must send him two hundred dollars; as, unless I did so, he might lose his farm.

I heeded the call, and sent him the sum. It was a hard trial. Parental care and affection, on one side, and my own interest, the love of the first money, I ever had the privilege of calling my own, the severe and hard labor it had cost me, and no expectation that I would ever receive it back on the other, balanced in my mind for a few hours. When I decided and sent the money, I felt relieved and happy. Soon afterwards I returned home with my fever and ague. I started on horseback, the common way of traveling then, and the day after, my chills, and the fever following, lasted eighteen hours, during which I could not sit up. I succeeded, however, in reaching my old home, having the ague every alternate day, on the way. Healthy air and kind attention soon restored me to health.

Returning to Salt Point in the fall, I again went to salt-boiling for the winter, taking my pay in salt. The usual pay was every fifth bushel, for boiling, or tending a salt-block. By severe labor and great economy, I saved and packed one hundred and twenty-two barrels of salt, by the first of May, which I owned. There was, by the laws of New York, a duty of five shillings per barrel on salt, which must be paid before it could be removed from the works. It was the duty of the superintendent of the salt springs to visit all the works and examine the salt, once or twice a week. By these visits, Dr. Kirkpatrick had often seen me, my work and my salt. I had no money to pay the duty on my salt, nor friend to assist me in shipping it abroad. I could not sell it at the works for cash without great sacrifice. What shall

I do? was the thought. I considered Dr. Kirkpatrick a gentleman. He had seen me all winter in that servile employment, and, of course, had no respect for *me*. He was made liable for the duty on all the salt inspected. To trust me was to become liable for the amount to the State. I was young, looking like a boy. Pondering all these things over, I concluded to rally courage, put on a good face, and ask the superintendent to trust me for the duty which was about seventy-five dollars, until I could take my salt to Canada, sell it, and return. I did so. He asked me how long I thought I would be gone. I replied, not over six weeks. Without another word, or the scratch of a pen from me, he wrote an order to Mr. Mead, inspector, to inspect and brand for me one hundred and twenty-two barrels of salt. He did so. The next day I had my salt loaded in a boat for Oswego, on the way to Canada. The mode of transit then was by boat twenty-four miles to Oswego Falls, freight, two shillings per barrel, a portage of one mile costing one shilling; in small boats to Oswego, twelve miles, two shillings, making five shillings freight to Oswego; thence, by vessel, to Little York, Canada (now Toronto), where I sold it, costing by schooner, one dollar per barrel, and half a dollar duty in Canada. I received pay in American half dollars, at which I was delighted. I returned in less than six weeks. The first thing I did was to take this shining silver to Dr. Kirkpatrick, and pay him the sum due. This was the proudest act of my life especially when I learned from him that it was my hard labor and good behavior that he had seen of me in the salt works, that gave him the confidence to trust me, while he had denied several merchants and other business men of the place.

I found by this that men of sense respected labor, and what I had foolishly supposed the superintendent looked upon contemptuously, was the *great merit* that gave me credit.

CHAPTER II.

The Author's Business History.

Having now fairly entered upon my commercial life, I continued once or twice a year to ship salt to Canada and the Western States.

The second winter after being of age, at Salt Point, I spent in a lawyer's office, studying law reports, the principles of law, and attending courts to gain legal information. It was the most profitable winter of my early life. That study prepared me to do my business writings, and fitted me to understand the legal bearings of commercial action.

There were no harbors on the lakes; no lighthouses, nor a steamer. The Western country was just beginning to be settled. There were but few, probably not a score of vessels navigated from Montreal to Chicago, and these were small sail craft.

I continued making, buying and shipping salt. My first shipment, to what was then called the Upper Lakes; the lakes West of Niagara Falls.

The transit I have described, to Oswego, thence by vessel to Lewiston; *portage* of seven miles to Schlosher, thence in boats to Black Rock.

There was no harbor at Buffalo. Vessels loading at Black Rock, were towed by oxen up the Rapids into Lake Erie. My salt was for Cleveland, Ohio, and having all of my means invested in it, I went *along* to sell it. The freight on this lot of salt was three dollars and a quarter per barrel—now about thirty cents. This was early in the spring of 1819.

The commissioners appointed by our government to establish the boundary between the United States and Canada, after the close of the war of 1812, were on the same vessel my salt was shipped on.

The vessel sailed directly to Detroit. I then shipped my salt and myself back to Cleveland in a small vessel called the *Hannah*, Capt. Belden. There was no harbor at Cleveland; no warehouse, and but a small village.

I remained some two months at Cleveland, endeavoring to sell my salt for money, but there was none to be had. Finally, I traded for a drove of cattle, driven from the South to sell. There was no money to buy them. I drove them to Salt Point, but there was no one who had *money*, to buy.

I grazed them in Salina reservation, until they were well fatted in November.

There was then no market, no butcher, no packer. I had to be my own. I sold the meat again, for salt; converted the hides into cash, and the tallow into candles, and peddled them at five pounds for a dollar.

I extended my business; purchased six hundred acres of woodland near the works; married, built a house on the land, and lived on it two years.

The year previous to this, I invited Dean Richmond (an orphan without a home, and cousin of mine), to come to my house and live. I urged him to give up his roving habits, live in my family, run the salt works, in which I would give him an interest. He did so, and he did well. I was then in mercantile business with a Mr. Barnes, and at my suggestion, Dean bought him out.

When the Erie canal was first opened, I bought a boat and horse, employed a boy to drive him while I steered, and took into Rochester the first load of salt ever taken thence by canal.

Syracuse had now grown into an active little city. Dean Richmond had grown by his application to business, integrity, and perseverance, a solid prosperous business man, with twenty thousand dollars. His talent as a boy, and as a man, was of high order. I had never borrowed a dollar, I had never asked assistance, had no friend to aid me, nor did any one, except the kind Dr. Kirkpatrick.

I was worth twenty thousand dollars before my name ever went inside of a bank for a loan.

In 1830, Mr. W. Williams, wholesale merchant in New York, sought a mercantile partnership with me, and took the interest of Dean Richmond. Our firm was "Richmond & Williams."

The new firm did a large business, selling goods, manufacturing and shipping salt.

In the early spring of 1832, I had occasion to go to Ohio, on business, without a thought of purchasing or moving West. Night overtook me at a country tavern in Perry, Ohio, a few miles from Fairport, the name of the little village and harbor of Grand River, thirty miles east of Cleveland. The common bar-room contained all the guests, and the liquor of the house. Besides myself, there were several persons from Fairport, one of whom told the others that it was intended to purchase ninety acres of land on the river opposite Fairport village, and lay out a new town.

Without inquiry, I learned by their conversation the quantity of land, its location, and that Judge King, of Warren, Ohio, some forty miles distant was the agent.

My business called me directly to Warren. I resolved to see Judge King, and make inquiry, thinking there might be an object in purchasing. At Warren, I called on him in the morning. I found that he had late the evening before, arrived from a long absence at Washington. A large number of letters had accumulated in his absence. He was indisposed to talk until he had read his letters. Then I made inquiry about the land, asked for its refusal until I could go and see it. He could not grant this; on his table were three letters, asking his terms for this land,—that he must answer these letters, with terms of sale, but if I wanted it, and would decide *then*, I could have it.

I had not seen the land, was traveling on business, had no thought of buying property in the West, when I left home,—"I said to him, I have only money with me sufficient for my current expenses,—am a merchant in Syracuse, N. Y.

If you will accept my check on Onondaga Co. Bank, I will take it, and you may make out the title."

Judge King accepted the proposition. In two hours the matter was adjusted. On this pivotal circumstance, in this country tavern, and meeting Judge King at the only moment that he was at liberty to sell the land to me, changed my location, and future career. My business life changed, I became a resident of the West.

Feeling that I had ever been controlled by a Providence, wise and good, it gave me confidence in all my future movements.

I saw the property and was pleased. My brother living in the vicinity, I engaged him to build me a dwelling and store-house. I returned to Syracuse, and informed my partner of my purchase, and my intention of removing to that place. he urged me to give him an equal interest, and continue our partnership. I assented. We sold our mercantile interests at Syracuse, and moved to Richmond, Ohio.

CHAPTER III.

Here in 1832 we commenced forwarding and commission business, selling heavy merchandise and paying cash for country produce, being the first cash market at that harbor.

My partner Mr. Williams removed to New York. He attended to purchasing goods for me, and selling the country produce I shipped to him.

This trade was daily increasing, settlers came and the town grew rapidly.

I owned stock and was director in the Bank of Geauga. My credit was unlimited.

Our business was very profitable. Everything was prosperous until about 1838. A canal was constructed nearly parrallel with the Lake, from Beaver, Pa., to Cleveland. This canal cut off the country trade to the Lake, from Richmond, Ashtubula, and Coneaut harbors, and transferred it to Cleveland, consequently all these places went down.

Each year we built one or more vessels for the Lake trade, and took a small interest in the steamer *Rochester*, when she was built.

In May, 1837, the financial crash came, all the Banks in the country simultaneously suspended specie payments.

This fell like a thunderbolt upon the country creating universal alarm and consternation. Suspensions and failures followed in quick succession.

The other owners in the steamer failed, and on me she fell with a debt of thirty-five thousand dollars. This, with my other indebtedness, embarrased me. A few creditors asked for securities, I refused them, and notified all, that I would secure no one, and that I would pay no *one* faster than I would *all*. I would pay any one in property on call, or if undisturbed I would pay every dollar and interest, in *cash*.

This positive course saved me from failure and loss of all. I had due me eighty thousand dollars, not five thousand was ever collected. We had dissolved partnership.

From the time of this suspension I ceased collections for lots sold. I felt the loss of business to the town by this canal, and the embarrasment of the time; the place was valueless for business, and that it was unjust to collect pay for what had no value.

These circumstances led me to rent my warehouse, discontinue business, and devote all my attention to the settlement of our affairs.

Pursuing my own course undisturbed by creditors, I had every dollar paid, with interest, before 1840, and a trifle over twelve thousand dollars left.

Early in 1835, I loaded the schooner *Hellen*, Capt. Chase, with provisions and fruits, for Chicago, to supply this small village. Directing the

Captain after he sold, to advertise, and run her as passenger packet between Chicago and St. Joseph, Michigan, until September; then return home. He did so, and in ballast, not being able to find anything for shipment East. The vessel returned as directed, and made a good season's business.

The people suffering under their embarrasments were very clamorous against the banks for suspending specie payments, in May 1837. The following fall, thinking I had some financial capacity, they elected me to the Legislature.

I was appointed one of the Committee on Banks and Currency. I found strong prejudice in the Legislature against the banks, the committee had no idea of other, than coercive laws.

Without the knowledge of any member, I commenced with the session, gathering facts and the history of the banking business of each state, and the United States, from 1810 to 1837. I wrote a report, and read it to the committee. It surprised them. They directed me to report it to the House, with the bill I had drawn, which I did. It changed the opinion of the majority. The House ordered five thousand copies printed for the use of its members, a compliment not extended to any other report that session.

The bill was passed into law, which enabled the banks to resume, and within thirty days from its passage, most of them were paying specie for their bills, although allowed over one hundred for that purpose. This received the commendation of financial and business men.

CHAPTER IV.

I removed to Cleveland, and connected myself with parties in Detroit, Buffalo and New York, in commercial business. We continued nearly three years. Our business was large, having charge of seventeen sail vessels, a daily line of steamers on the Lake, and thirty-two canal boats on the Ohio canal, running from Cleveland.

In the winter of 1843-4, my head clerk bought the interest of the other partners. He and myself continued the business two years, when I determined to dissolve, and remove West.

When I closed with this partner, I left in his hands, assets of nearly one hundred thousand dollars, to settle liabilities of about sixty thousand, all being matters of the firm. Instead of converting them and paying the indebtedness, he took another partner, continued business, using the assets as capital, and died; leaving these debts upon me, which I subsequently settled, never receiving a dollar.

Before leaving Cleveland I purchased the schooner *Swallow*, 110 tons burthen, for my son, Charles to take into Lake Superior. He did so in April,

1846, hauling her one mile overland, around the Falls of St. Mary's River, on timbers and rollers, then launching her.

This was the first vessel on that lake. It was needed for the copper mining business just commenced along its shores

Two years before, I assisted my eldest son to establish himself in mercantile and commercial business with goods, vessels, and store-house in Racine, Wisconsin.

I spent nearly a year searching for a good business location in the West for myself. Better pleased with Chicago, than any other place, on the 12th of April 1847, I bought the warehouse on the corner of State and South Water Streets; again engaged in the shipping, forwarding and commisssion business, dealing largely in country produce.

Chicago had no canal, no railroad, no telegraph, and but about fourteen thousand inhabitants.

My sons engaged in business with me, the two oldest being silent partners. The firm was "Richmond, & Co.

The first ten years we were very successful, accumulating nearly three hundred thousand dollars in property. Having started an active business, my vision began to penetrate the future, and contemplate a much larger trade for Chicago.

Standing on this "Pisgah top" of commercial prospect, considering the immense country spread out between us and the Rocky Mountains, and surrounding us on either hand, scarcely a tithe of which was cultivated, the product of which must find its *first* market in Chicago; but its *ultimate* in *foreign* countries by way of the sea; I saw the New York Canal inadequate to the coming demand.

Looking further, following the waters of Lake Michigan through Huron, Erie, Ontario, and the St. Lawrence River, to the broad Atlantic, I perceived the proper channel, the one that God had made for that purpose, and that we must avail ourselves of, in coming time. Southward rolled the mighty Mississippi. Fortunately thought I for the country, these two channels existed.

The latter was ours; unfortunately the St. Lawrence was in *British* possessions, where our shipping might not pass or trade, until the right was secured by treaty.

Inspired by these considerations, and to open this great channel, I wrote a series of articles for the "Chicago Daily Commercial Advertiser," urging the importance of the free navigation of the St. Lawrence to *both* countries. Many of these articles appeared in Canadian Journals, and were copied in the English papers.

I corresponded with Sir Hamilton Merritt, of Canada, who acted as Colonial Secretary; he favored the object most earnestly. I endeavored to arouse the West to the advantages of this river to our shipping interests. On presenting the matter to Senator Douglass; he saw at once its importance. Taking the facts and statistics that I had prepared, he successfully carried the measure of a reciprocal treaty with Canada, through Congress. Thus was secured this great boon ; the free use of this river.

In the autumn of 1854, the Free Soilers, Abolition and Whig parties fused, and formed the Republican party. A number of its leading men addressed me, asking my consent to run for the Legislature.

I replied by letter that I would accept the office if elected, and fill it to the best of my ability, but it must be done without any effort on my part ; that I regarded offices created for the benefit of the people, and they aught to decide who should fill them uninfluenced by any effort of the candidate. Besides this, I felt too much delicacy to solicit votes for myself,

I was elected, and appointed by the Speaker of the House of Representatives, Chairman of the Committee on "Banks and Corporations," a very laborious position. This Committee had the fullest confidence of the House, its reports and recommendation were generally adopted without much opposition. The respect and kindness exhibited towards me by the members of that body was more than I expected, which gave me much satisfaction, and excited gratitude. Here I formed a close acquaintance with the genial Abraham Lincoln, subsequently President of the United States.

CHAPTER V.

In the summer of 1855, I commenced building a Hotel, and rented it for ten years from its completion, to Messrs. Tabor, Hawk, & Co., who opened it September 1856, and called it the "Richmond House." It continues to bear that name.

It cost without the land, a hundred and forty thousand dollars—eighty thousand above the estimate of the architect, when commenced.

Meanwhile, myself and son Charles were building a large vessel in Cleveland, Ohio, for the Lake and ocean trade, between Chicago and England, *via* the St. Lawrence. She was named "Dean Richmond," and loaded with wheat in Chicago, and sailed for Liverpool, August 1856, my son master and supercargo.

The first voyage that was made between these two ports direct. We made the experiment more to prove the practicability of a direct commerce between the Western Lakes and foreign countries, than hopes of private gain. It was eminently successful, accomplishing the voyage in sixty days, without accident, delivering her cargo in good condition to consignees.

We sold the vessel in England.

Holland, my son and partner,—my dependent for assistance, being confined by protracted sickness, the whole of our extensive business devolved on me. It was too much for my body and brain. However, I sustained our business until the close of that year's navigation.

The opening of 1857, found me prostrated. I abandoned business and took my room unable to do anything. In May following, I left Chicago for the home of my childhood in Vermont, remaining the summer upon the farm where I spent my yonth. In September, I returned with improved health.

During this absence the great financial crash of 1857 came, and appalled the country. All kinds of property were offered for sale, but there were no buyers. Suspensions and failures followed, and distress prevailed. We had lost much in grain, vessels and insurance.

The eighty thousand dollars cost beyond the estimate of the architect for the Hotel, also the failure of the Hotel rents, and other moneys due us, together with our depressed business, and maturing bills, compelled us in 1858, to seek a loan.

I sought an old friend and capitalist in the East, in whom we had the fullest confidence, and arranged with him to furnish what money and assistance we needed to sustain us.

In order to secure him amply, and make him feel cheerful in aiding us, we gave title deeds of our real estate, intended as mortgage security, with all our assets in stocks, bonds mortgages, and otherwise, and sent the same to him in New York.

He kept and used all this property, without fulfilling any part of his engagement, and refused to answer our letters of inquiry—unscrupulously holding these titles to our property without giving any consideration whatever.

Subsequently this man died, the administrator of the estate refused to notice our claim. To obtain justice, we commenced suit against the estate in the United States Court, for two hundred and fifty thousand dollars, which is now pending.

In April 1858, I made arrangements with the president of the New York Central Rail Road Co., to act as agent with my sons, for that company and the line of steamers running to Chicago, in connection therewith.

This business furnished us support while we held it, six years.

While engaged in this agency, I purchased and shipped to Eastern markets annually, large amounts of flour quite successfully. The profits enabled me to purchase a block of five houses on Park Avenue, to buy some stocks, and relay the North Western Plank Road, which was worn out and nearly valueless, a majority of which we had owned since 1848.

We transported the material for the government steamer *Michigan*, from Pittsburg to Erie, Pa., by canal and lake.

We transported the first iron bars laid in the Michigan Central Rail Road, by that state from the Ohio River to Detroit.

The first ties laid in the Galena and Chicago Union Rail Road (now North Western), were furnished by us, and brought by our vessels from Ohio.

Our vessels were the first in Saginaw, and did the exclusive carrying trade of that place for several years.

The stone in the first built Court House, being the centre of the present extensive building, we brought from Buffalo in our vessels.

I first suggested the formation of the Chicago Board of Trade, and with a Mr. Whiting, who was made the first secretary and was the first grain broker in the city, called the meeting and prepared the plan and papers for its organization.

Before there was a steam vessel on these lakes, or government constructed a harbor, or built a lighthouse along these shores—before any canal was made or telegraph contemplated, I commenced commercial pursuits upon the Western waters, and have followed the same for more than half a century.

For forty years I applied myself full twelve hours each day, and for twenty years managed a larger business than any other person in the Lake trade, without one month's recreation. Fifteen years of this time in New York; fifteen years in Ohio; and twenty-three years in Chicago.

The Western country has grown to its present position, entirely within my observation, and some of it through my humble services. Fifty-five years ago my first journey to the West, Utica, N. Y. was the most Western town of any magnitude and trade. Tide-water supplies were taken by teams from the country to the Hudson River. Along the Mohawk the roads were thronged with loaded wagons for Albany market.

Anxious to know the laws of life and health of my own organization, I made it a study in early manhood, and have endeavored to obey those laws as I discovered them. For more than forty years I have not drank a glass of spirits as a beverage, and have abstained from intoxicating drinks of every kind.

After using tobacco over forty years, in 1860 I gave it up, and immediately added to my weight nearly thirty pounds.

I uniformly retire before ten in the evening, and rise early. Whether at home or abroad, I aim to have my meals at regular hours, and eat nothing except at mealtime. With few exceptions, I have enjoyed excellent health; and do at the present time.

I have lived in the most interesting period of human life. At no age of the world has mankind developed their faculties so rapidly, and made such rapid strides of human genius, mental growth, and spiritual manifestations.

I write this brief narrative of my more prominent business career, not to exhibit myself, but as a basis for this book, which claims to be of *Divine origin*; showing its author to be a plain, practical, business man.

Here, at the close of this short narrative of the leading events of a long business life, I desire to make a few suggestions for the benefit of young men, and those in business, more advanced.

I can say in the language of King David, "I have been young and *now* am old; yet have not seen the righteous forsaken, nor his seed begging bread."

To young men I have to say that your reputation is entirely within your own keeping. Character and reputation, are not exactly the same, but they are very nearly akin. They are a better capital for you than money. They will carry you through life, and furnish you a better close of it than wealth.

But you may have both; seek first the former, and by industry and prudence, the latter is sure.

To business men I have to say, you feel that you can manage and control your own business, which is true to a certain extent in ordinary cases.

You cannot control the great events of the country, which are all-powerful in their effect. I have lived through three periods of great national and universal embarrasment, that of 1817, 1837 and 1857, besides the many minor embarrasments the country has felt. In each of these cases many men who felt, and whom the people thought sound and wealthy, had to yield to the general pressure.

My experience and observation leads me to advise all business men, that when these pressures come not to make sacrifices of money to pay maturing debts, not to secure any one to the prejudice of other creditors; *but keep your means for the benefit of all creditors alike.* Suspend, before making sacrifice.

Many a good man has failed by paying shaves, and tying up his means by securing the more clamorous creditors, leaving themselves powerless to settle or compromise with other creditors.

CHAPTER VI.

The Author's Religious History.

Having given a brief narrative of the leading incidents of my business career, I now give an equally brief relation of the leading and more important movements and incidents of my religious experience.

Under the term religious, I include motives, object, sentiment, faith and practice,—moral, political and pecuniary; indeed all springs of action.

My parents were religious people, members of the Congregational Church, good representatives of the Bible, my father of the Old, and my mother of the New Testament. Father's administration habits, were after the manner of Moses. Mother's after that of Christ's—attraction. Father remembered that oft quoted passage "spare the rod and spoil the child."

Mother governed her children by the beautiful tender law of love. She was filled with loving active goodness. My father was a good man.

At about four years of age I was taken with the other children to a neighbors, where there was a religious meeting and many children of the neighborhood were baptised. One circumstance leads me to remember it. After one child was baptized, while the venerable old minister (whom I thought was God) was invoking a blessing, I ran up to him to be the next.

My parents were rigidly consistent with the puritanic morality of New England.

They brought up their children in the nurture and admonition of the Lord, as they understood it; especially was my dear mother a Godly woman, not only pious, but "pure, and of good report."

In my formation, she gave me a religious nature, —in early life, religious instruction. I have never forgotton her hand upon my head, the prayers uttered, the blessings invoked, and consecrations of me, to God, to justice and truth, time and again.

I can never forget her earnestness in teaching me of God, of His love, His goodness, and Christ's care for little children. In my twelfth year, she left earth for her heavenly inheritance.

Not long before her departure, she stated to her family, her faith as to her coming life. She believed that she should be a *living conscious being* in the Spirit-World, that she should still remember, love, and visit her family. That she would know their sufferings, their joys and sorrows, and the thoughts of their hearts, and be able to administer comfort to them. I have been conscious of her guardianship during my whole life, since her departure.

Often when temptations beset me, and darkness shrouded me, have I felt her gentle, sweet, angelic monitions saying, "this is the way, walk ye in it," my child, and in obedience to them have I been blessed and happy.

Every member of the family deeply felt the loss of the wife and mother. All felt stricken and bereaved. Our young family suffered a loss that could not be repaired.

At about ten yeags of age, I heard a sermon that my mind retains to this hour, from the text, "Jacob have I loved, but Esau have I hated."

The preacher read the context, and deduced the doctrine of Calvin therefrom, to wit, that before the world was, God elected some to salvation, (a certain few that could not be increased or diminished by any possibility), and doomed all the remainder to everlasting suffering in eternal fire, with the Devil and his Angels, without respect to anything they had done, or could do, and this to manifest His power and glory.

This sermon gave God so bad a character that my young mind could not accept it.

My mother had taught me that God was love, and repeated to me many Bible passages of the same import. I could not conceive that a just God, a God of love, *all love* should create a race of conscious beings to suffer in eternal burning, without abatement or hope., just to show *His power*, or how He could manifest *His glory* by such an act.

There probably is not one in a thousand that will

read this book, that knows that this is the doctrine. The Westminster Chatechism, and Presbyterian articles of faith, that the New and Old School Presbyterians adopted as their faith, in coming together as one body in the year 1869.

Probably not one in ten, of the members know that this is the *basis doctrine* of their church, or that their minister before he could be ordained, had to affirm to this "doctrine of Devils"—the conception of tyrants—and *never* the doctrine of the Bible.

When Methodism was introduced, I remember well the excitement in that vicinity.

The Congregationalists regarded it a fatal heresy, and opposed it accordingly. Meantime a sect grew up under the auspices of Elias Smith, calling themselves "Christ–ians." This doctrine was new, and was preached and sustaned with ability. The Adventists of this day, are a product of that sect They were not specially opposed.

Meanwhile the Universalists made their advent, proposing to save all mankind. It was all Heaven—no Hell. Against this doctrine all other sects were united in their opposition. It would never do for God to save *all* mankind!

I am inclined to repeat, and show the doctrines of all these sects as understood there.

The Congregationalists were Calvinists, holding the doctrines of the sermon just referred to, unconditional election and reprobation, irrespective of works.

Methodism proposed to save all that would accept Christ's atonement and live good lives; the rest to suffer eternal burning.

The Christ-ians proposed to save all that would comply with certain conditions, and annihilate the rest forever, burning up "root and branch."

The Universalist's doctrine saves every human being. In this attitude each church or sect, raised their banners, inviting the world to the embrace of their faith, and the fellowship of their church. To join the Congregational Church was saying, I am one of the "elect."

To join the Universalists, was saying, God will take care of his offspring.

Joining either of the others, was saying, we will try. Such was the presentation of sectarian religion to the people in New England sixty and seventy years ago.

Our family was forbidden at first, to attend the Methodist meetings. An appointment of preaching in a barn near us, attracted me to it. I feared my father's displeasure. I watched the preacher intently to catch something heretical to repeat to my father, thinking that it would divert him from my disobedience. Happily for me he never referred to it.

All these religious sects increased for the time, those that were opposed *most*, grew the fastest.

The Methodists have now absorbed the Congregationalists, and their house of worship in the town where I lived, and more or less in adjoining towns.

I was young when these things were transpiring, with little opportunity of gaining general knowledge,—was a simple farmer boy. As far as possible I became acquainted with the religious sects here described. I respected them all, and especially the one to which my parents belonged.

CHAPTER VII.

In 1817 I settled in what is now Syracuse. N. Y., and not until ten years passed had I any serious religious impressions. In the winter of 1827, I lived on my farm, three miles north of Syracuse. There was great excitement among the people. They had a protracted meeting in the village, and a great revival in progress. We were visited almost daily by some minister or religious person calling our attention to the subject of our soul's salvation.

These extraordinary efforts impressed us solemnly, and the result was, I experienced a spiritual birth. What I understood Christ meant in his saying to Nicodemus "the wind bloweth where it listeth, the son of man heareth the sound thereof, but canst not tell whence it cometh, or whither it goeth, so is every one that is born of the spirit."

This I realized then, and do now. I felt then as now, the great truth of a spiritual birth

Meantime my wife had a similar experience.

Now, each of the different churches that had interested themselves in us, sent their articles of faith for our consideration, but to their credit not a word of persuasion or proselyting was uttered by any one.

My study of the Bible was constant and searching. It was for spiritual truths, the knowledge of God's laws, His ways, and of a future life. I was hungry for spiritual food. I did not study doctrinal points at all. I was attracted to the Presbyterian Church rather by reason of my social relations, than otherwise. After a few months examination and reflection, we joined that Church, which is now in the first ward of Syracuse.

In 1826, a pamphlet was handed me containing a lecture on temperance, stating how fearfully the use of spirituous liquors were increasing, and its havoc in making drunkards. This was the first movement in the great temperance effort that spread through the country.

At that time I became interested in the cause, signed the total abstinence pledge, and with others formed a temperance society, the first in that vicinity.

This was the year previous to my religious exercise, when I joined the church. The total abstinence pledge then taken, I have never violated.

It was not popular with the religious people or the clergy at first, they stood aloof from it, but in time came strongly into its support.

In 1832 we moved to "Richmond," Ohio, at the harbor of Fairport. Being the owner of the land and that embrio village, I felt a solemn responsibility regarding the settlement, its religion and morals. My religious and temperance principles over-riding all other considerations.

I refused to sell or lease lots to any person to sell liquor on, and inserted a prohibitory clause in all titles given to lots sold,—criticising every man's principles that proposed to settle there. Determined to protect my family and others from the contaminating influence of intemperance and profanity. My rules were very rigid and positive, nevertheless, they were popular in the religious community. They attracted such as I desired, and repelled those I did not.

The first year I built a large school-house, which served our purpose for religious meetings for a time, all parties using it.

The second year we formed a Presbyterian Church, with eleven members. I was chosen Elder, and George Everett Deacon.

Clergymen of all denominations visited and preached to us occasionally, making my house their home. Soon, Methodist, Baptist and Episcopal Churches were formed, all having preaching more or less of the time.

At the first, we arranged a Sabbath-school, Mr. Everett being superintendent. We organized a Bible Class, I was chosen teacher. The rules of our class was, that no commentary should be used in the study of the Bible. The members were limited by this rule to their own resources. **Nearly all** the adults became members of the class.

Our Bible studies were very rigid, continuing a subject from week **to week,** until thoroughly investigated.

The subject of King Saul ar.d the Woman of Endor (called the Witch of Endor), was under examination for several weeks increasing in **interest** at each meeting, and at the last, there was no house large enough to hold the people ; **it was held** in the spacious saloon of a steamer that **was laid** up in the harbor.

This Bible Class **pursued the closest study** of the *Jews*, their origin, nationality and life. This more than any previous, **experience** established my political sentiment.

It taught me that *God goverrned nations.* When the Jews obeyed His commands, **they** prospered. When they disobeyed, they went into captivity and suffering. I learned that it was as important for a nation to do right—be just, as for an individual.

This study led me to see, **and feel more** clearly **our nation's guilt in** sustaining **slavery.** From this time I looked for a retribution from God's hand upon this guilty nation.

Nearly all the population became members **of** some of the churches.

The village was famed for its religious and moral principles.

In the absence of preaching we kept up our

Sunday meetings. I usually conducted them by reading sermons or other religious matter that was found instructive and agreeable. The people were all very Catholic in their feelings, worshipping together, in harmony.

The fourth year, the congregation having outgrown our house of worship, I sought to raise money from it, to build one for all parties.

This plan was not acceptable and was given up. Then with my *own* means, I built a church of good dimensions, and finish, for the use of the Presbyterian Church. The society employed the Rev. Mr. Fitch, to preach to us. Our new church was well filled by earnest hearers. On extraordinary occasions I lent it to our neighbor churches.

One occasion of this kind offended our minister, which he never fully overlooked in me. The Methodists desired it for an important occasion on a Sunday, and not being able to consult the minister, I let them have it. Feeling that my relations to them, as well as my good feeling, demanded it. I owned it, and let the Presbyterians have it, and why not the Methodists?

Although there were four churches, there was no sectarian antagonism. A wonderful harmony prevailed. The religious people enjoyed a growth in christian graces seldom experienced. They were happy and cheerful.

When I meet any of them *now*, they are sure to refer to their enjoyment while living in Richmond, as being the happiest of their lives. The Catholic spirit prevailing there, drew the people together in social relations, destroying the spirit of strife.

About 1835, Rev. Albert Barnes, a Presbyterian minister of Philadelphia, author of Barnes' Notes, preached a sermon denying that the posterity of Adam were personally guilty of his sins, but admitting that they inherited Adam's nature, and as a consequence became sinners by reason of the sinful nature of the parents.

Rev. Professor Judkin took exceptions to the doctrine, and complained to the Synod of Philadelphia. (I write from recollection.).

The case was appealed from this tribunal to the General Assembly of the Presbyterian Church of the United States, to sit in Pittsburg, Pa., in May, 1836. Mr. Fitch our minister, and myself, were appointed by our Presbytery to represent it in that High Ecclesiastical Court. The Assembly was full. and great interest was felt. Dr. Judkin the prosecuting party, said in his complaint and charge, that if *Dr. Barnes' doctrine was true, it destroyed all his hopes of salvation.* The trial lasted several days, and was closely contested. It was decided by a vote of that body, acquiting Albert Barnes of preaching heretical, or unsound doctrines. I voted for the acquital of Mr. Barnes.

The following year, the General Assembly of the Presbyterian Church at its annual session had a majority of Old School, or of Dr. Judkins' party, and they voted a separation, or rather excluded from their body all the *New* School, or the party sustaining Mr. Barnes. These bodies called the Old and New School, remained separate, each having its own organizations and meetings. They remained so, until the year 1869, when they again united, adopting as the doctrine of the Church, what is commonly known as the *Westmin-Catechism and Paesbyterian articles of faith,*

Slavery was the *real* cause of their separation, —its destruction—their reunion.

CHAPTER VIII.

When I moved to Cleveland in 1840, I joined Dr. Aiken's Church, (New School.) This church was very large, and the next year a colony went out from it and formed the *second* church. This society employed Rev. Mr. Canfield, pastor. I was one of the colony, and remained in the church until I moved to Chicago in 1847. From my earliest apprehension of truth and right, I hated injustice, especially in the character of oppression or extortion, which hatred grew with my growth, and strengthened with my years.

In 1831-2, the public and religious mind was aroused upon the subject of slavery in our country, and its great crimieality. I learned that the "American Colonization Society" which was patronized throughout the North as an institution opposed to slavery, was really in its interests.

That its object was to protect slavery by removing and colonizing *free* negroes who disturbed the quiet of the *slave*. I became an abolitionist as necessarily and promptly as the mercury rises in the thermometer in heated air. *My religion compelled me* to denounce slavery and the colonization society, and to advocate the abolition of that "sum of all villainies." What seemed to me should be the sentiment of every Christian and upright man, was not. Hence, to my astonishment, I found the church and people ready to crucify abolitionism, and they did mob, egg, stone and abuse the advocates of justice between the negro and his master. I hope American History will do justice to the shame and degradation of American Christianity and the people's sense of justice. *I charged then, and now charge American religion with the crime of American Slavery.* My judgment *was*, and *now is*, that had the American Church at any time, in more than two centuries of its life, unitedly set its seal of condemnation upon it as a sin, and turned the religious influence against it, twenty years would have peacefully emancipated every slave in America.

But instead of this, more than half of the American Church defended it as a *Divine* institution, pleasing to God, and a large portion of the remainder apologized for it. American Slavery in all religious aspects sat in Moses' seat. Each General Assemby of the Presbyterian Church, was very careful to distribute positions equally to slaveholders and others. Careful to appoint a slaveholder to administer either the bread or wine at the Lord's Supper,—tender of her as of youthful innocence. In the church—my office—my business and in my politics, I labored against slavery and in favor of abolition, for many years.

But no *efficient* decided action was taken by the embodied New School Church against it, while the Old School sustained it with all its power.

On coming to Chicago in 1847, I brought letters from the church at Cleveland for myself and wife. She joined the Second Presbyterian, Dr. Patterson's church. I declined. I was visited by Dr. Patterson and by the elders of the church, invited and urged to join it, but *I could not do it.* The reasons in my own conscience, and those I gave those good friends were the complicity of the church with slavery, giving it countenance sinfully, by communion and fellowship with it, while condemning it in weak and wordy resolutions. *Under these circumstances my conscience became positive, and my judgment and heart responded.*

I could not believe that God approved it, or that the Bible sustained it. I could not see how one could do by others as he would like to be done by, and hold a man a slave. To me it was overwhelmingly unchristian to make man—property. If slavery was right then the negro might own his master or me in other circumstances. I hated slavery with a perfect hatred.

Subseququently, I wrote to the church session in Cleveland, that in justice to it and myself, I felt bound to advise it of my course, knowing that the rules of the church held me as a member, responsible, until I joined another. That death, or some violation of its rules, were the only means of my discharge. Therefore, that I might not cumber it, or its rules, I stated the course I had pursued and the cause of it. That in view of which the session could do with me whatever seemed proper under these circumstances.

Nevertheless, I continued to attend Dr. Patterson's church, observed religious duties and privileges as formerly. My faith, hopes and aspirations remained unchanged for the time.

CHAPTER IX.

In the winter of 1848, what was then termed the mysterious rapping near Rochester, N. Y., occurred. I heard reports of their movements in what they called spirit communications, at first with indifference, then growing hostile, for a time opposing it. At length my daughter-in-law Carrie, boarding with us, was developed as a medium. We respected and loved each other. After many solicitations on her part, and seeing the small stand move about the floor, and writing through her hand, my curiosity was awakened occasionally to look at the movements. I had felt and said that

"I have an established religious faith touching future life. I have no confidence in these manifestations although I cannot account for them. I choose to rest in my present faith undisturbed." Notwithstanding, she would offer something every opportunity, and occasionally very impressive phenomena. In the spring of 1854 she visited her parents in Buffalo. Soon after this on my way to New York, I called upon her at her father's. Carrie proposed to show me some manifestations. I declined, and as I left, I felt that I had been abrupt in my reply, and turned back, thinking that I would silence her, by imposing a condition that would baffle her. I said, Carrie, if there is any spirit that can convince me that they can come and manifest themselves, Mrs. Chester is the one. Get her spirit to come and I will attend to her; supposing this impossible, and that her failure would end her importunities.

(Mrs. Chester was sister to the late Dean Richmond.) I had known her from infancy, through a life of severe experience, had been her advisor and confident. She was a person of talent and force.

Returning at evening to tea, Carrie met me playfully, and said, "father I have agreed with Mrs. Chester's spirit, to meet us at Mrs. Baker's this evening; she is my sister, and a better medium than I am."

After tea, Carrie, her mother and myself went to Mrs. Baker's. Sitting in a long parlor, Mrs

THE AUTHOR'S RELIGIOUS HISTORY. 53

Baker brought a light stand, and sat down before me, placing her hand upon it. Immediately the stand rose up and tumbled itself on two legs into my lap. Said I to Mrs. Baker you have managed that stand very adroitly, in getting it up here, and I not see how you did it. Instantly the stand walked off some fifteen feet, so I could observe everything done, and rolled and toppled round with only Mrs. Bakers one hand on it, and often it would rock away from that hand. This seemed to say to me, look and see if Mrs. Baker does this with her hands. Then the stand walked up to within a yard of me and stood still. Mrs. Baker says to me, ask questions; the stand will give three movements or tips for yes, one for no, and two when neither yes or no, will correctly answer the questions. For the moment I sat confounded, under the reflection that possibly the immortal spirit of that dear friend was present, prepared to respond to me from the eternal world. For a few moments there was not a question in my brain, nor a word on my tongue to utter. At length recovering myself, I began questioning of our childhood, our school days in Vermont, and brought in our religious experience, joining the church at that time. More than forty years experience was included, extending my questions as far as possible, and so that yes or no would give an intelligent answer. I spent two hours with no other word spoken than my questions. So far as I knew the facts, the answers, every one, were correct, and from this fact, I presumed that *all* were. When I had done, I had no more doubt that the spirit—the intelligence of Mrs. Chester had responded to my questions than I had of my existence, nor have I since. I believed *then*, and *now* believe, that God appointed this means for my convertion. That He sends angel messengers to men, to do his will and execute his purpose.

This was an important and a *pivotal moment with me.* An hour destined in its results to change my whole life. *I could not help believing. I was convinced throughout my whole inner nature. All my faculties were captured. I saw that the veil that separated this from spirit life, was rent in twain,* and *through the opening we meet departed spirits face to face.* That instead of the theories of spirit life gathered from tradition and the Bible, we might now have the *facts, the actual life experience* of *disembodied spirits*, with nearly the same facility that we could learn life in France or Germany. Here I halted, I hesitated, I wondered in amazement. The seal was broken, the book was opened to me.

I feared error and delusion above all things. I thought of the wiles of Satan, and the many warnings of the Bible, again I would review this experience, always finding in it conviction and confirmation of the fact. I had no *power* to disbelieve, *conviction was rivited in my soul.* In this condition I endeavored to strip myself of every preconcieved opinion. I called to my aid the bible teachings for obtaining truth and guidance. I was as honest as Daniel and sought the truth in the same way, by prayer and suplication; and as to him, so the light came to my mind; the answers came in the same way, and I came into the rest of faith in due time, without wavering.

The next desire after getting over this struggle, was to learn *of the life of spirits, and that state of existence.*

One evening in May 1855, I came home from business and to my astonishment, Carrie was entranced and the spirit talking through her to a sick son. I sat down near by her; she turned to me with face and expression radiant and shining, and commenced conversation with me. The voice was sweet and gentle—intonations kind and loving. The spirit purported to be a female; she reviewed my religious ideas and habits of judging others, my lack of considerate charity for those thinking and believing differently from myself.

In my whole life, I was never so rebuked, chastened and subdued as under her gentle exposition of my faults, and never so profited by teaching.

She said at the close, " When you come to the spirit world, I shall be your companion, and will be with you while you remain here, as your guide and support." I think she has been, and is with me as I write this experience. I named her, " Venus," and this fifteen years we have been friends and familiar companions. I recognize her presence most clearly. This was the first time that Carrie was entranced, of cource the first time she ever spoke under entrancement. It was the first time that I ever saw an entranced medium speak, and it was the first time Venus had ever used a medium to communicate to mortals. For these years we have carried on a correspondence through Dr. Farnsworth a writing medium by which I have gained great light.

Carrie having developed into a trance medium, we had sittings for development, manifestations and teachings. We had now reached 1856; early this spring at a sitting, a spirit spoke most beautifully through Carrie to us; at the close, she turned to me and in a kind tone of voice, asked me to form a permanent circle in my house with my family, and any of our neighbors having good intentions, as desired to be with us. The spirit told us that he would preside at our circles. In reply to my inquiry for his name, he said it was *truth* he wished to communicate, and chose to give it for its own sake and upon its own merit, without the influence of a name, but at some future time would give it.

Then we commenced a circle, sitting once each week, and after a few months, they were so interesting we held the circles twice a week.

After some few months Carrie went to Buffalo to visit her parents again. After an evening of very brilliant action as amedium, reetired to rest at about eleven o'clock and never awoke to consciousness in the form; all signs of physical life disappeared about eleven A M next day; physicians said she died with disease of the heart.

Our circles at home were continued for more than a year. Soon after Carrie passed away, Mrs. Tipple was sent us from Rome N. Y. by the invisible powers.

Some six months or more after we commenced our circles, the controlling spirit announced his name John Quincey Adams. I fully believed it was him; the sentiment and management of the spirit side of the circle indicated a person of ability and experience. We enjoyed these sittings exceedingly, through this more perfected medium. A great variety of manifestations were given, various and many conditions of spirit life were exibited— physical mental and spiritual, from the exalted and happy, down to the low degraded ones, in the darkness of ignorance, and those suffering in the hell of sin; Mr. Adams giving explanations and significations of the movements. He seemed to aim to give us all information possible, both by langugae, illustrative of physical manifestations, and tableaus. Every effort seemed made to impart knowledge to the circle.

Up to this time Mr. Adams apparently had only sought to convince the circle of the great fact that the spirit of man continued to live through the separation of the soul from the mortal, and retain all the faculties posessed in human life. And further to establish the fact, that under favorable circumstances they could communicate to us.

He had carefully avoided touching church doctrines, *until he had secured every faculty of my mind* to unwavering belief so far.

One evening I invited in some presbyterians to see and hear. Mr. Adams took occasion to attack and demolish the whole system of orthodoxy, and the plan of salvation as preached by the clergy. I was exceedingly mortified that he should take that occasion when these friends were present, to attack their faith and mine; for the first time I reproved him for so doing as unkind. However, I said to him, if our faith is wrong, please give us the truth as you find it practically revealed in the world of spirits. He replied, that the next Friday evening he would commence, and continue on Friday evenings until he had given us a system of truth as uuderstood in spirit life.

This he did to the satisfaction of the circle; but our presbyterian brothers did not attend to hear it. Up to this time I had never investigated theology closely for the Bible evidences of the various creeds, and doctrines held by the different churches. I had sought only to live a christian life, and do a chaistian's duty. I inherited my religious system of faith from my parents; they taught me practical religion in my childhood. I accepted their faith as I should their farm—without questioning their title.

An ever-present fear of embracing error led me to the closest xamination of the teachings of Mr. Adams and also of the Bible. I confess for a time

I was in a great strait. I had a severe struggle over this subject. I was "betwixt two"; an old conceded doctrine, supposed to be taught in the bible—believed by nearly all who claimed to be christians, and was venerable in age. On the other hand was the spirit of that true, venerable patriot and practical christian John Quincey Adams, many years experience in spirit life, dwelling in light ineffable. Old belief and sentiment asserted one class of facts as truth;—the spirit of an old well known high-minded man comes direct from the Divine effulgence and states an opposite.

There was nothing left for me but to clear my mind from all choice and influence, and again seek truth from God, the only source, as Daniel did.

With the most ardent desire for eternal truth, I gave all my faculties and powers to its acquisition. I could do no more; my soul was soon satisfied, and faith came by hearing. In my inner soul the still small voice established belief. This was not of choice. I had no other desire than to obtain the exact truth. It established itself within my susceptible nature. When the soul seeks truth, and makes itself receptive, it comes as a necessity; —God is pledged for it. And "when you ask bread, will he give you a stone? When you ask a fish will he give you a serpent?"

Not only in these circles, but in every way possible, I sought to test the truth of spirit manifestations.—for occasionally a cloud would envelope me It seemed so wonderful that the supposed dead should talk to us. Whenever I came in company with a medium, my spirit friends would take occasion to communicate some test and confirmation of its truth. I believe that some spirit guardian was always with me.

During the winter of 1857, while confined by sickness, a spirit claiming to have been a German Protestant minister, visited me in my room frequently, through the medium Mrs. Tipple, and gave me much satisfaction as to truth and practical spirit life. He then, twelve years since, told me that I would be the author and publisher of a book that would be translated and published in many other languages, of precisely the character of one I am now preparing for the press.

My life had been an active, practical, business life, without any thought or pretentions to literature or authorship. I was faithless of this prophecy. Through him and others, almost the entire acts and career of my subsequent life was foretold to me. This German minister was very intelligent and interesting. I talked with him frequently and familiarly as I do with a friend. I told him if it was designed by spirits to develope me as a medium, I preferred unconscious entrancement. He says, in substance, "No, that is not the design. You are a man of business experience; you have been many years upon these lakes; you are known as a business man, almost from the ocean to the Rocky Mountains. This experience and acquaintance render you of great value to the cause. You are being developed for use in your apparent normal condition."

I was constantly, in season and out of season, in search of truth, of light, and facts touching the spirit-world and life therein. *"He that seeks shall find!"*

In the summer of 1857, I met with the then leading, and very prominent medium in Boston, John M. Spear. When introduced to him, he held my hand and, while entranced, delineated my character perfectly. I spent the summer in New England, and much of the time in my sister's family, who were Methodists, but soon became Spiritualists under the evidences and manifestations produced there.

There was a few substantial, active Spiritualists in the vicinity, and surrounding towns, but in this town there was little knowledge of it, and *that* was the scurrilous and false reports circulated by ignorance and enmity.

My enthusiasm on the subject, awakened much interest. The people being aroused, got up meetings, and something of a revival ensued. Many persons with strong prejudices, yielded them when they fully understood what Spiritualism was, and accepted the doctrine as truth. A great change of sentiment followed the spread and explanation of this new sentiment.

There is nothing so difficult to deal with as ignorance. It is the home and source of prejudice. The knowledge the ignorant lack, is supplied by prejudice and bigotry. This otherwise intelligent people, were ignorant of true Spiritualism, consequently deeply prejudiced against it.

Late in the fall of 1858, through the hand of Mr. Spear, I was invited with several other persons, to meet in Boston on the first day of Jan., 1859, by the Spirit Congress, for the purpose of devising a plan whereby the consumers of the East and West might retrieve themselves from the horde of speculators that taxed their supplies by large profits of trade.

The parties met. A tangible plan was formed, simple and easy, which was for each town and city east, who consumed western products, to associate and organize,—make up a capital sufficient,—appoint their man to manage it at home,—then all the towns unite in one agent at Chicago to purchase, and ship direct to each location whence such body was formed, thus saving a large per cent. that speculators made by the ordinary course of trade. The agent at Chicago by controlling so large a trade, would be able to buy supplies in market, and ship them direct to the consumer at the lowest possible rates, and for a very small commission; and, also, to ultimately apply the same rule to a returning trade from the East to the West.

The plan was never actualized. Money was scarce, and persons in the towns and cities were distrustful of success, fearful of agencies, and unwilling to get into joint responsibilities. The invited persons remained in Boston during the winter. I was there about ten weeks,—long enough from the Divine Mind. I think the papers from him will sustain the declaration.

This was not my first interview with him. While in Vermont in 1857, and in Boston in 1859 especially, were his visits and communications to me frequent. At other times Dr. Franklin has impressed his presence and thoughts upon me, and when available, and mediums were present, he would speak to me. I was quite familiar with him in this way for some years before this agreement was entered into.

About this time, a Mrs. Merritt, a medium from Michigan, a stranger to myself and family, came to my house. She said she had a mission to me, and every morning under influence, she manipulated my right arm. She said it was to preserve and prepare it for a work that would be written through it, of more value to the world than any book now published. She remained about three weeks, magnetizing it every morning.

Whether this has had the influence or not, I cannot say, but my arm and hand are now as steady to write at seventy-four, as they were at thirty-four years of age.

There was an eminent physician in Philadelphia in 1776, a member of the convention who signed the Declaration of Independence, "Benjamin Rush.' He was a man of force and ability, and is now an efficient spirit, pursuing the same profession. Mediums, especially those engaged in healing, and many Spiritualists are quite familiar with him. In the winter of 1860 he wrote to me that he had chemically examined my person, and discovered it badly charged with the seeds of disease,—that the thoracic duct was entirely closed, and the system loaded with diseased matter; and without immediate attention I would be prostrated. He directed me to take a tea spoonful of raw Alcohol mornings before eating, and on going to bed take as much as I dared, mixed to suit my taste, which I did. Five weeks later he gave another examination, and wrote me that he found the diseased ducts greatly reduced, the closed duct cleared of its matter, but advised me to go to Salem, Mass., and take a course of Alcohol and fruit baths, which would be given under his directions,—Dr. Franklin approving of the same. I went and took seven baths on successive days. They were of heat and vapor issuing from burning Alcohol and various tropical fruits

Those baths were given me in the morning in my room. My breakfast and meals through the day were of the most nutritious kind. I have ever felt that this treatment was of great value to my future health.

The philosophy of it was this: The baths and sweating forced out the old disease and morbid magnetisms which had accumulated in the system and was effecting its secretions; that the rich, fresh and nutritious food furnished a new and fresh supply to take its place. Hence, in about seven baths the system would be cleansed of the old and supplied with the new and more healthy substitutes.

CHAPTER X.

My life's experience has rendered me self-reliant in matters of business and sentiment. As the Bible directs. I have called "no man master," or "Lord."

I admit no authority over my reason or conscience, but the Divine Mind; neither wealth, fame or position commands my esteem when goodness is wanting. In my mind, goodness in man alone constitutes greatness. Jesus Christ was great in goodness, so was Washington and Lincoln.

Nevertheless goodness often excites intense hatred. How the Jews hated Christ! How the Southern people hated Lincoln! Both were assassinated by hatred.

When I became free from human bondage and sectarian faith, never investigated, and went to the Divine Fountain of truth, without respect to anything else, and committed my faith and ways to God, asking and trusting Him, *light came*; pouring its rays upon the Bible revelations, nature's revelations, and an inner light came, surpassing all light that I had ever received.

The good old prophet Daniel taught me much. His earnest determination to gain knowledge and guidance from the invisible world; his persevering n fasting aud prayer twenty-one days, and until "the appearance of a man came" and gave him the knowledge he desired,—visions, symbols and spirits were given him in reward of his determined perseverance. His interest was so strong it drew to him the desired truth, and he accepted as truth what came, and proclaimed it. An honest-hearted man desiring and seeking for truth above all things, for its real worth, having no prepossessions, cannot control his faith, and ought not.

Such a man in process of time, will find the truth built up within him as a natural result. *God is pledged for it.*

If such a man tries to believe in Methodism, Calvinism, or Spiritualism he is no longer honest to himself or true to his purpose. If honest he wants the exact truth, whether it *proves either or neither of these* doctrines. He accepts what comes to his inner soul. In his earnest search after truth, Daniel believed what the spirit said. He wrote it, and it is accepted by the church as a revelation from God.

The churches use the same Bible. Each minister reads it in view of his belief, and the creed of *his* church. They understand the same book and text differently. Why? Simply because their church doctrine is their standard of truth! Now they cannot all be right! and probably none of them are.

Aspiration induces inspiration. Truth comes to the aspiring mind according to its development, direction, and the earnestness with which it is sought.

CHAPTER XI.

The communications from spirits that follow this chapter, are copied from the originals which I have. I have given a brief narrative in the preceding chapters of a few of the leading events of my life, up to the commencement of these letters, and the experiences connected with them.

They cover ten years,—beginning with the year 1860, the election of Mr. Lincoln President, and closing with 1870, when the revolted states having returned to loyalty, and the Government is reconstructed.

During these ten years, I have been a public medium. Of my mediumship and my acts as such, I have said but little in the preceding chapters,—prefering rather to let my labors as such be inferred from the communications made to me from time to time during these years.

The communications which follow are such, and only such, as pertain to the war of the rebellion alone, while they are but a small part of what I received during these ten years.

When the reader has fully perused all of these messages, and contemplates those not published, and realizes the fact that I have been obedient to every requirement therein made, he may judge somewhat of the labor I have performed.

The past five years have been exclusively devoted to, and under the direction of the powers above. These messages have been my guide. I have obeyed them fully,—while I have felt free to go and come, as directed by Dr. Franklin. There has always been an irresistible pressure or power upon me to obey directions, which have been to me God's call,—*His will*, working in me, in the law of attraction. Yet sometimes, when hesitating, as I have occasionally, St. Paul's expression, "Woe be unto me if I preach not the gospel," would come to me with great pungency, and determined my course.

Under these directions and others, I have been fourteen times to New England, in the years including 1859 and 1869, beside going to many other places. I have also, attended four sessions of Congress since the close of the war,—during the period of Reconstruction, Amendments of the Constitution, and the adjustment of our Government. During the trial of President Johnson,— and also, the inauguration of President Grant, his cabinet and administration, I *was specially called upon to be not only in Washington, but in specific places*. During Johnson's trial, I was required to be in the Senate Chamber. While President Grant's administration was being organized and put in working order, I was directed to be at the White House, or in my *room* most of the time.

By the same promptings, I have written scores

of letters to Presidents, Members of their Cabinet, Members of Congress and Governors of States from time to time, pressing the principles of equality and justice being extended to the colored man,—some of which will appear in these pages.

The careful reader of the following messages to me will learn my mediumship and the use the powers above have made of me, and why they have required faithful services on my part.

I was not required to talk, or externally manifest. *It was to think, to be a battery of brain, mind and thought* through which spirit minds could act on other men's brains,—transmit mind, thought and sentiment. Hence, I was required to be in the Chamber of the House, or Senate, where, and while the reconstruction measures were being considered, during the four sessions of Congress that I was directed to attend.

Unless to some person who could comprehend my use, I never named my business in Washington,—appearing only as a spectator of the scene.

Senator Wade accepted the idea of my mission. Senator Howard accepted the general idea of spirit influence and control,—and so did a large number of the Senators and Members of the House of Representatives, to whom I did not disclose my mediumship. Occasionally some individual understanding my mission, would wonder at my faith, remarking that they could not be so governed. One reply answered for all: "Very well, it is not for you, but it is for me."

CHAPTER XII.

*Communications from the Inner Life,
With Notes by the Author.*

This chapter contains the war communications from spirits to me. The following is the first one directly relating to the coming Rebellion. Although a rather indefinite prophecy at the time, it was, however, significant of coming events. It was written soon after Mr. Lincoln was nominated for the Presidency, through the hand of John M. Spear, in Cleveland, Ohio, and sent to me at Chicago by mail.

OF THE CRISIS.

Cleveland, July, 1860

Dear Sir:
The present may be looked upon as a most perilous moment,—several things may be looked at. There may be internal darkness, as there has been an external eclipse; one connects with the other

The political horizon is ominous of a season when parties will not know where to look, much less how to act.

Should the union split, as in a short time it may, all business will be at once deranged, and the wisest commercialists will be perplexed how to act.

All Europe is in a most unsettled state, and the conditions of things there must soon affect and disturb the more solid stock markets of the United States.

There is a general expectation in the public mind, that some marked events are at hand, and the more shrewd classes will feel that non-action is safer than action.

The associated Spirit-world are acting in various ways to so unsettle, or disturb the public mind that a new and better state of things may come into life.

You are now cautioned how you move at this present moment, and for the next few months. You will soon be informed of certain things of a national character, which will much interest you, and you will clearly see how the New Jerusalem is to descend to earth, and bless the human kind.

From your old friend,
John Quincey Adams.

In the fall of 1860, a few days after Mr. Lincoln's first election, he came to Chicago. I felt impressed to call upon him at his rooms. I said to him, "Mr. Lincoln, you will be assassinated!" He replied, "What makes you think so?" I said that the South was not satisfied with his election; and in the two instances before, that they were dissatisfied—Harrison and Taylor, were both poisoned soon after taking their seats. I advised him to be careful who he had about him, and who prepared his food. After a moment's reflection, he said, "If they are determined to assassinate me, they will do it." His journey to Washington in the winter under disguise, (by timely warning given,) indicates the truth of a living intention to take his life, even before entering upon the duties of his office, and the truth of my prophecy.

Sunday, April 28th, 1861, a medium entranced in my house had this message given through her to me:

"There is a most diabolical, hellish plot about to be acted upon, to kill Gen. Scott, and Lincoln. Life is in great jeopardy! Jeff Davis is a black-hearted ruffian, and will stoop to any villiany. The Southern leaders will do the same!

A. Jackson."

This was given by Gen. Jackson, Ex-President of the United States.

Early in the spring of 1861, I was directed by Dr. Franklin to go to New England. In obedience, I was in Manchester, N. H. in June, and at a private house where I was visiting, there was an excellent medium, Miss Barrett. On Sunday morning, about 10 o'clock, she was entranced. Her spirit seemed to leave her and go to the Spirit Congress, then in session. She was made to know many of the spirits. The subject of the Rebellion was then under consideration,—and as one after another expressed their views, she repeated to me what each one said.

Of the large number present, Washington, Adams, Franklin, Jefferson, and Patrick Henry all spoke, in the most positive terms, that there could be no compromise or concessons. The crisis had come, and Slavery must be abolished! She repeated the words after the speaker to me, but I made no note of them, I only recall some of the interview, and the positive manner of the speakers and the conclusion.

In the same fall, I was again directed to go to Boston in December, which I did, and on the 21st, Dr. Franklin requested Mrs. Pamalee, Mrs. Lull and myself to form a circle at the house of Mr. Parmalee, that should be permanent. Accordingly, we formed "the circle of three." This was done in the presence of a large concourse of spirits, sixty-four of which gave their names and desired a record made of them, which I now have. Several of the former statesmen of this country addressed us, and gave us the reason why the circle was wanted, and its use. It was said that we three persons had the elements when combined to make a powerful battery for spirit use, and they expected to use this battery on the Administration. They directed that the circle meet every third Thursday, evening in a certain room in Mr. Parmalee's house. Mrs. Parmalee and Mrs. Lull were both mediums of control and clairvoyance. To my suggestion, that I could not be there at those meetings, that I should be in Chicago, Dr. Franklin said that they would dispense with my presence, but I must sit by myself at home, at a corresponding hour, fastening my mind upon the circle with all the interest and force I had. This I did. At the hours appointed, Mrs. P. and Mrs. L. recognized my spirit present with them in the same manner, and as distinctly as they did disembodied spirits.

At the formation of the circle, these ladies both saw the spirits and heard them give their names, and express the interest they felt in the circle. At each sitting a great number of spirits were present,—especially those present at its organization.

In Boston I received the following communication:

June 9th, 1862.

My Friend:

You are an instrument in the hands of a wise power, and soon you will realize the magnitude of your usefulness to the beings of earth. You are to meet with the circle at Mr. Parmalee's while here. Give it due attention. From that circle much good will come. When the conditions are more favorable, I will give you through this medium, the knowledge you desire. In this matter you have much to do, and it will be within your reach to not only benefit others, but to be of great service to mankind.

Your guardian, *B. Franklin,*

Early in August, 1862, I received the following letters in one package, from Manchester, N. H., with a note from Miss Barrett, saying they had been written through her hand, and that she was directed to send them to me. Each differed from the others in the hand writing, although there was some similarity. This mediumship in her was not strictly and wholly mechanical, nor impressional. Both hand and brain were used to produce these letters.

THOMAS RICHMOND—
My Dear Friend:

You have set your heart on the acquisition of wisdom that cometh from above. You have sought also for a universal love that embraces all of God's humanity. You have not sought kingdoms, nor houses, nor office; you crave only the chance of doing all the good you can to God's children.

Now, for all these goods in thy soul the Father's good pleasure requires us to send you before the mighty ones of earth, to speak such words of wisdom as shall be given unto you. So much we reveal unto you to-day. The head of this nation is in perplexity and doubt. He has consulted many in the form and many spirits,—some of them he has followed. If he would go to his room alone, and listen to the voices now so anxious to speak to him, he would hear in his inmost soul, the voice of the Great Eternal, calling him to let the slave go free; for I see from this plane of vision, that if he don't heed his ways, the whole country is under a monarchial government. Let every one who truly loves liberty and equal rights, exert himself in this cause.

You, sir, are one that I look to in this great emergency, to carry out the principles that you profess. I ask you in the name of Justice, Liberty and Truth, if you are ready to go forward as a second Daniel, to the Babalonian King, called the United States of America, whose President says he will stick to the Constitution, and is sticking to it, although it has one plague-spot upon it, which *must be ruled out*, or, by the Eternal, the United States, President and all, will be ruled out for many centuries to come!

Your Friend,

A. Jackson.

MANCHESTER, July 30, 1862.

My Dear Friend Richmond:

Thee will see that we are anxious for thy co-operation in our grand plans, nearly ripened. The country needs true patriots.

The time has come for thee to exert thyself for the cause of Freedom. Thee will be obliged to try thy mettle with the President. Thee knows already that much depends upon thee. Thou art preparing for thy work, and art now ready for some of it. We give thee warning, through a channel that is running thy brain and heart, that thou must follow orders. Thee will have much influence on his mind. He must follow his convictions, or the whole power goes into other hands. He needs thy sympathy and presence, when a certain measure shall be brought before him for consideration. Thee will feel modest, Friend Thomas, and somewhat doubtful, like thy old namesake, whether it is the Lord that sends thee. We say to thee, words of wisdom will be given thee when the time comes to speak them.

Thee must point him to the hand writing on the nation's wall. If he don't let Africa's children go free, it is a doomed nation;—if he don't listen to the Daniels that we have raised up to interpret the hand writing on the wall.

Mighty events are just upon ye. Every individual must use all their will-power over the President and his Cabinet, and leading officers in the Army. Wrongs in high places must be exposed. We see in secret, but have no suitable channel to speak through to the President. Many of the people think that some of the leaders are inncompetent. They are willing to fight for freedom, but they want officers to lead them that are honest. There is too much selfishness in headquarters, and it shall be exposed!

I have much more to say to thee, but will wait for another favorable time.

I will help thee often in thy labors of love.
Thy friend,

I. T. Hopper

July 29th, 1862.

Vive la Libertie! March on! March on! Let your souls be resolved on liberty or death. To arms! To arms! ye brave!

Joan, of Arc.

The sun of the nation's destiny will set in darkness if we cannot arouse the true friends of liberty! March on! March on, to the City of Washington and do our bidding there!

Josephine.

Fair Sir:
From my home in heaven, I come to the loved ones in the form,—and strive to give you courage for the coming storm. Arise! my beloved, arise! You belong to the great and wise. Fear not the hangman's halter, nor the headsman's block. I am with you in the work for God and Liberty!

Mary, Queen of Scots

You must cross the Alps for liberty,—head and heart!

Le Empereur,

Napoleon. *

In November, 1862, I received a letter from Dr. Franklin's spirit, through the hand of Farnsworth, requesting me to be in Boston early in December.

I received another near the same time, from John Quincey Adams's spirit, through John M. Spear's hand, requesting me to be in Boston by the 12th of December following. In obedience to these calls, I arrived there about the tenth day.

On the 17th, Dr. Franklin gave me the following, and continued until the last day of the month.

These messages follow in their order:

My Dear Friend:

Conditions are more favorable for me to communicate to you than before. It is my wish that you should write to me every morning, as it assists me to communicate to you. I control this medium in such a manner that it is not possible for his mind or feelings to color the thoughts that I wish to convey to you. I have intimated to you before, that you are to be the means of doing much good to the beings of earth, and that your mental powers are to be used as the principal agent in developing a new phase of medium powers.

I wish you to remain in Boston a week or two longer for the purpose of receiving spiritual influences and communications.

To-morrow morning I will give you another message through this medium.

Your Guardian,

B. Franklin.

December 18th.

According to promise I communicate to you this morning. It is my wish and intention that you should visit Washington at some day not far distant. The American people are now suffering for their past sins. The present conflict which exists between the North and South could not be avoided; and in the eyes of Him who seeth all things, your civil war is but a just retribution to the beings of your country.

Spirits of power hold the destiny of your country in their keeping. We can favor no party feelings,—but must act justly by all. We must act in conjunction with our heavenly Father, in order to wield a protecting power over you.

The object of the present war is being accomplished; still, the people are to experience more intense suffering in order to bring about the desired result.

You are to be used to confer with the leading magistrate, and dictate a plan which must be acted upon in order to bring about the highest good of the country. At the closing up of the civil war, you have, as an instrument in the hands of spirits, an important work to perform in bringing about a just settlement.

My object in thus intimating this to you is that you may be prepared for the work and hour in view, and by this disclosure to you, it enables us to act upon your brain with more efficiency. You will bear in mind that spirits control your war to a great extent, and it is within our power of action to suspend hostilities when it is best

Your past leading statesmen still hold a controlling influence over your people,—as when in the form. You will soon receive directions to go to Washington, and confer with the leading men of your Government. A plan will be given which you are to lay before them, and they will be influenced to act upon it. Give yourself no uneasiness in relation to your finances, as you will be amply provided for in every direction.

It is my wish that you return home before you go to Washington.

It will be some weeks, before you commence your labors with the government officials. I shall soon disclose to you the plan you are to act upon in order to bring about the desired result.

I wish you to place your mind as much as possible upon the affairs of your country, as it will aid us in preparing you for your future labors. *Franklin.*

December 22nd.

The cause of your present national difficulty is what I wish to speak of this morning.

If Slavery had never existed among your people, the present civil war would not have taken place. Consequently, Slavery must be entirely abolished before peace can be established between the contending parties of your nation.

Though in eradicating this poison from your people, it may be the means of nearly bringing destruction to your government,—still it is a necessity and it is God's will that it should be done, and other spirits of power with myself, are commissioned by the Father of the Universe to remove this curse and stain from your country that you may be the chosen people of God from amongst all the nations of the earth.

It was through spirit influences and control that we possess over the beings of earth, that your present conflict was first agitated. We have maintained our control over the affairs of your country, and shall continue our supremacy until peace, harmony and right prevail.

It may appear to you that so much sacrifice of human life might have been avoided. We were compelled to act upon the leading passions of the people, in order to bring about justice. We have more power in bringing about the desired result in causing your people to slay each other than by resorting to any other method. It is God's will, and His laws must be maintained. He waited sufficiently long to have the North and South abolish American Slavery. It could not be done by influencing the minds of the people to abolish it, by holding councils and discussions.

Your nation could not discover that justice and equality to all mankind was their due,—consequently the people must be compelled, and suffer for past wrongs. You have tasted but to a slight extent the sufferings that will come upon your nation before the matter is fairly settled. There are to be severe battles and great destruction of life, before the cause of your calamity is removed. You have been selected as one of the principal agents to confer with the chief magistrate, to have a settled and fixed plan adopted for the North to act upon, by which peace will be ultimately restored,—and those who are true to God and his principles, will be carried through the trying ordeal, and be victorious in their efforts.

The time has come to act more directly upon the leaders of your government. Your President is impressible to spirit influences. He has been made to change his feelings in relation to the affairs of the country, as it was best that he should. But he will be made to maintain a firm position hereafter, through the agency of spirits acting directly upon him by means of yourself and others. To-morrow morning I will communicate more concerning your country and your mission. At present let your mind keep as cheerful and hopeful as possible, that I may accomplish that which I intended before your visit to Boston. Your Guardian,

Franklin.

December 23rd.

My Friend Richmond:
The spirits that communicate to the beings of earth, especially those that took an active part in

the American nation when they existed upon earth, and were leading minds of your country, are now directing all their influence to your national difficulties. Seemingly we are paying but little attention to other matters for the present.

The first labor that you will perform under spirit influence, and make manifest the power that we give you, will be in producing a change of action and feeling among the leading statesmen at Washington.

Consider that this power which will be given you comes from God; that He has selected you as an instrument to fulfil His promise to the people, and keep them from destruction.

The treatment that the first settlers of your country exhibited to the natives, the Indian race, was not in accordance with justice. Your people allowed this feeling of tyranny to develop itself, until slavery was established, and *now* slavery would be the cause of exterminating the American nation, were it not for the action of God's power and mercy upon the people.

I foresaw this national calamity when I first entered spirit life. I have been preparing for the crisis, and through God's goodness and wisdom am invested with power to guide your people through this distressing conflict. It is necessary that nearly all the national resources of your country must be resorted to, before our plan of bringing about a just settlement between the North and South is accepted by the Government, as we wish the majority of the American people to realize the magnitude of spirit power—its elevating tendencies upon mankind, and the happy results that will follow a true progressive life upon earth. When this object is attained, then we have supreme control of all organizations which now exist; we can then exert our influence in all the departments of earth life, and raise mankind nearer the Divine light. Then the prevailing influences amongst you will be peace, harmony and justice, and you will become strong as a nation.

I communicate this to you that you may perceive the real condition of your land, and comprehend the only course to be pursued in bringing about this reformation, so that you will be prepared to set forth to those persons with whom you will soon hold audience, the bearings of the case in such a manner that the desired object will be obtained.

I shall instruct you on all necessary points before you visit Washington, so that you may be invested with sufficient power to carry out our designs. I am also impressing you, preparing your mind for the results upon the leading politicians, to be effected through you, as an instrument. Then you will turn your attention to the social world; in fact, the entire condition of mankind and its relations as they now exist, will be changed for the better. Before this takes place, however, the nation must suffer intensely.

Those who are true to God and His teachings,

will be invested with power to destroy the evil which now exists among you.

To-morrow morning I have something more to say of your national troubles; then I shall speak of your development, and other topics necessary you should be acquainted with.

Franklin.

December 24th, 1862.

My Dear Friend: The subject upon which I have been communicating, that of your national dfficulties, I wish you to confine your thoughts to, and *give it all the attention possible;* and if there are any points that you do not comprehend, I will explain them to you.

The reason of my enjoining upon you a thorough and comprehensive knowledge of your national affairs, is, that we can operate with greater ease upon you, and through you as an instrument, produce a more decided impression upon those persons who occupy position, but at present are not disposed to yield to the highest laws of their being, and pursue the course that God desires of them.

I wish you to become conversant with the form in which you must act upon those persons, *as your medium capacity, which is peculiar to yourself,* is of such a nature that it is important that you should be accessory to all the knowledge concerning yourself, possible. You are at present what the beings of earth term an impressible medium. That phase of mediumship is one of the most satisfactory forms of spirit development to us, because the brain of such a medium is like a delicate harp—which we may boldly touch, to bring forth every note it can produce.

This harp is so encased and concealed by means of spirit influence brought to bear upon it, that its separate chords will be as music to those who can receive it, because it proceeds from Divine inspiration. Other sciences may have fascinations for their votaries; but there are none so fascinating as this form of mediumship to a well-balanced and progressive mind—none that appeals so directly to the laws of your being. This form of impressible mediumship you are to use in your association with other minds, but in connection with this, you are to have a new phase of mediumship under your immediate control and direction, which you are to employ to bring about certain results. In order that your medium capacity should increase, it is necessary that you should mingle with persons who are congenial to you. It is my wish that you should associate mostly with females, as you receive from them a magnetism which increases your power.

You also receive impressions who to be with—your impressions are reliable in that respect.

It is necessary that you should regard these conditions, so that you may arrive at that plan of action that God desires of you.

Consider that your first course of action with the President and others, will be to use your impressible power—that is, we will impress, you during your audiences with them. Besides we will impart to you a plan through this source, that you are to show them, which they will be compelled to act upon. We will also give you all the directions necessary for you to accomplish the object of your mission to them.

You are literally an exchanger, as you are the one selected as bearer of despatches to the head of your nation, and through you we will illuminate the leading men of your government with a plan of action that will rescue your country from destruction. I wish you to read this communication several times as it will serve to direct you in your future course. It is my desire that you should make all the inquiries you wish, before this series of communications is ended.

Your Guardian,   B. Franklin.
December 30, 1862.

My Dear Friend: Your mission to Washington is to give to the President a plan of action that we shall give you through this medium after your return to Chicago. Through your organism, we shall impress upon the mind of the President the importance and justice of this mode of bringing your national matters to a settlement. Carrying out this plan will be the first step taken in producing a change in your national affairs, and effecting the desired result. We shall also through your means make him feel the necesity of adopting it. In fact, your national affairs will be in such a deplorable condition that he will be made glad to receive your plan of action, and will heed it.

Consider that before you go, you will receive all the necessary instructions regarding your mission to Washington, and you will fully realize the power which is given you, and feel within yourself the ability to produce the change in national matters that you desire.

You are to tell no one who originated this work for you, but let it appear that it is from your own individual resources.

I do not wish you to say one word to the President in relation to Spirit Philosophy, or what you term Spiritualism. It is my wish that it should be understood by the beings of earth that it is your plan, and that you are the author; as, owing to the present condition of public sentiment the plan will carry greater weight and take stronger hold upon the minds of the statesmen at Washington.

You thus perceive that it is through you that we produce a general influence over the future destiny of your nation.

You will also perceive that the manner of action which we have dictated to you, owing to public feeling, is the only course to be pursued, to make the nation accept our plan for the adjustment of your present troubles.

In some of my future communications to you, I will be more explicit on this subject. I think some person will accompany you to Washington, but cannot say positively, as it is not time yet to arrange that matter.

In regard to my authority for disclosing to you that you were appointed by God for this mission, I can only say to you now, as the question, in order to make you understand the answer in all its bearings, requires a lengthy explanation, that God communicates with the beings of earth directly through gradations of spirit life, and has the power of selecting those who can do the greatest good to his creatures.

I will speak to you of the Divine Mind in some of my future papers. All these important questions shall be made clear to you but I am compelled to take them in their proper order.

You will perceive the workings of the Divine Mind in the same way that I do. The assurance of ultimate success in relation to your mission to Washington, comes from the Divine Source, else I could not reveal to you the method of procedure.

Dr. L. L. Farnsworth has been selected by a powerful circle of spirits as your principal communicator. It is possible, however, that others will be appointed to aid you, and will be used as mediums in connection with your future labors. You may rely on this medium as the one through whom I can best express my wishes and will to you. You will not remain long at Washington, as it will not be necessary to make a prolonged stay on your first visit.

    Your Guardian,   *Franklin.*

At the close of this series of papers, I returned home to Chicago, not fully comprehending their import, (While these papers were being given me, I was receiving an equal number of scientific papers also.) The language was clear enough to my understanding, but the selection of myself for this work, perplexed me. Passing by learned men, statesmen, jurists, and politicians, and thus selecting me of all Americans, a business man, to carry forward a work of this public character and magnitude, I deemed strange in Infinite Wisdom to do—a Power whose vision penetrates all the secret springs of life—motives of men, and measures their ability, integrity, and purposes. I could not realize my fitness above all others, to control the leading minds and measures of the national government, although well acquainted with the President. At this early day I did not realize my mediumship as being of the extent and character that the spirit congress did, or as of sufficient importance to be used, as results have proved it to be. In a subsequent paper, Dr. Franklin gives his reason for not continuing the messages to me through the month of January, 1863, as suggested.

BOSTON, Feb. 5th, 1863.

Dear Friend Richmond :—The following is the commencement of the plan which your present national difficulties must be settled by.

I wish you to study it attentively until you

acquire a thorough knowledge of the subject that I lay before you, and if there is any part which you do not perfectly comprehend you are to write me at once and I will explain; you will perceive the necessity of paying much attention to those communications, as they will be of much importance to the beings of earth.

There is no other way through which you can emerge from your present troubles than by a recognition of the manhood of the colored race; by this I mean, in the ordaining of Providence, the right which the negro sustains in the scale of being, to his claims for freedom, for justice, and humanity.

God can never smile upon a nation, can never give permanent prosperity to a people, who ignore this immortal truth —*the right of one man is the right of all men.*

God is no respecter of persons; all are alike entitled to an equal chance, to a common inheritance, from the great Fountain of the universe.

When a nation ignores this, it is but sowing seeds, the fruits of which shall seal its doom. In the name, then, of humanity, in the name of a broad and unerring philosophy, in the name of the universal brotherhood which God has designed from the foundation of the world, should be established — *Give the negro an equal chance with the white man!*

Free and arm all the negroes in the Border States and that portion of Louisiana which you now hold in your possession, and send them forth to cut their way to freedom, and free their brethren who are now in bondage, and raise them to the position which the Great Father has decreed that they should occupy. There is no other way to your national triumph, to your national peace. This important lesson the nation has been slow to learn — this great principle has been so long ignored, that it may be too late to bring speedy salvation to your country, but in the grand working out of results, this course shall carry you to a position over which the angels shall exult, and man shall rejoice.

To-morrow morning, if possible, I shall again communicate to you. *Franklin.*

February 21st, 1863.

My Friend Richmond: — Conditions have been such that I could not control the medium until this morning. In this communication I shall endeavor to impart to you the entire plan in connection with what you have previously received.

The sooner your government wakes up to the emergencies of the hour, the better; by timely action it may avert the calamity which threatens its entire overthrow. New complications and obstacles are looming up in the distance.

Indeed, some are at your very doors. There is the South ready in the last extremity to offer freedom to her slaves, if they will take up arms against the North, rather than be conquered by you. The South will certainly do this.

Again, there is danger from foreign interference. France is keeping her own counsels, but is laying plans for future operations, which may startle the North like the shock of an earthquake.

The breach between the opposing parties at the North is growing wider, and threatens to culminate in fratricidal warfare and bloodshed.

How shall these evils be arrested? Only by *immediate and vigorous prosecution of the war, by the government's availing itself of every possible instrumentality in its power. By arming the negroes wherever they can be reached, as rapidly as possible; and by discharging all officers who are not really in earnest in the work of crushing the rebellion.*

You, my friend Richmond, are invested with influence. Let that influence be at once exerted in urging upon the government the necessity of active and vigorous measures. Go personally to Washington, if need be. Seek an interview with the President, and present to him the subject in detail, which I have here given you in outline.

Let Justice and Freedom be the watchwords now and henceforth. Justice and Freedom are *immortal!* They are backed up by the God of Hosts, and whoever plants himself in the way of their advancing steps, will be ground to powder.

The reason of my not continuing these communications daily after you left Boston, was in part owing to the medium's not being in a fit condition, and from other causes which I cannot explain at present.

It would assist me much if Mrs. Lull were to sit with the medium. Conditions will be made favorable for me to control him for weeks to come, but soon I intend to bring him to you at Chicago, as I can control him much better near you. You will hear from me again in a few days.

Your Friend and Guardian, *Franklin.*

At this time I was in Chicago. Mrs. Lull was in Boston, holding the "circle of three" with Mrs. Parmalee at her house, at the appointed times. Being impressed that a letter from me to Mr. Lincoln would be as well as a visit, I wrote the following letter to him, which Dr. Franklin said served the purpose quite as well as a personal visit would have done.

CHICAGO, March 2d, 1863.

Abraham Lincoln, President: — I am most deeply oppressed with the condition of our country, and impressed with the importance of such speedy action as promises to end the national strife, and secure the approbation of heaven.

Sir, had slavery never existed in our country, civil war and strife had not been. While the cause of the war exists, peace can never come. The elements of strife must be removed, or strife will never cease.

The perils of the hour are imminent. The sooner the government awakens to and realizes them, the better it can, by timely action, avert the calamities that threaten its overthrow. New complications and difficulties are looming up in the distance; indeed, some are at your very doors. I will name a few. Sir, you can see the constant weakening of public faith in the success of our arms, and the stability of our government, by that never-failing commercial thermometer — the price of funds, the relations that bank and national credit bear to coin.

You perceive, sir, the mercury of difference rising every week, until one dollar in coin will buy one dollar and seventy cents in government issues, and you may depend that there is more gold now being bought and stored away for personal safety, than when it was but ten per cent premium. This sinking of public faith must be arrested; public confidence must be restored or at least strengthened.

Again, the breach between the opposing parties of the North is widening. There is a very formidable minority in the North that acts like brakes upon the wheels of government, who sympathize with and aid the rebels in every possible way. There are persons amongst them who would pilot a hostile fleet through our blockading squadron into Southern ports, if possible.

There is danger, too, from foreign interference. France is keeping her own counsels, but is watching events, and laying plans for future operations, which may startle the North like the shock of an earthquake. The war she is carrying on in Mexico is furnishing a fine covering to a preparation for Southern aid or interference.

Then, Sir, the South is ready in the *last extremity* to offer freedom to its slaves, if they will take up arms against the North, rather than to be conquered, and *the South will do it!* Then the terrible consequences that will follow, none can predict.

The term of service of a large number of our troops now in the field has nearly expired; there can be but little done towards replacing them and increasing our force by volunteers.

Now it is my solemn conviction, that to subdue the rebellion and save the government, that special means must be inaugurated within one hundred days. What shall they be — what course will avert the danger?

I answer, first, by the government's availing itself of *every possible instrumentality to weaken the South*, and by the most vigorous prosecution of the war; by discharging from his command every officer, high or low, who is not really in earnest in crushing the rebellion; leave not a man in command, who is not loyal and true to the command of the President, and every measure of the government, and is animated by a spirit of conquest. Arm every negro slave who can be animated by the hope of freedom and justice, and promise freedom to every slave who will fight for it, no matter whether in loyal or rebellious States. Press with all possible speed the securing of the muscle and sinew of the slave population. It is *this* which will decide the strife between the North and South. That government which secures this physical power, and renders justice to the negro race by giving to it freedom, obtains a moral force that shall sweep before it all opposition. God demands the freedom of the slave; it was for this end He instituted this strife, and the side which shall liberate, and thus recognize the manhood, the equality before the law of the negro race, will strike into the line of *right and justice*, and secure the favor of God, and succeed in its aims.

Sir, unless you give freedom to the slave and arm him *speedily* the Confederates *will*; as sure as the North gains a few successes, Jeff. Davis will free and arm the slaves against us.

You thus perceive that the power of the North is in the sinews of war — the money; and *that* is based upon confidence in the success of our arms; confidence rises and falls as prospects are. Tested each day by commercial action, the public faith is now seventy per cent below absolute confidence in our success. Now, Sir, your position is an exceedingly responsible one. Upon your action depends the whole question of life or death to the American government.

In my humble opinion, Sir, the following course is altogether the most speedy and likely to succeed.

Promise the entire slave population freedom in the event of the success of this government in subduing the rebellious South. Let the rallying cry be *freedom, justice*, and *manhood* for the colored race. Secure the enlistment and arming of negroes as rapidly as possible ; put them under humane, vigorous and loyal officers, and let them cut their way through the opposing rebellious elements as rapidly as possible. Make a large call under the conscription law, and infuse a mighty vigor into every department of the public service.

Allow me to say in closing, that the negro race has been the element and cause of this strife, and the power of that race in its bone and sinew, will be the power, that, in co-operating with one or the other parties, will become the successful party. The negro race, armed and fighting with the South for freedom, the Confederate States may well put the government at defiance.

Our government, with its resources and armies, with the slave population as allies fighting with us, stimulated by the hope of freedom, manhood and justice, may bid not only the South, but all of Europe, defiance.

Hoping and trusting, dear Sir, that what I have said may not be offensive, but prove of service to you and the country,

I am Yours Most Truly,
Thomas Richmond.

From February to August I received no communications from Dr. Franklin upon the subject of the war. My directions came through my own impressibility, as the medium's condition would not admit of his being used for these war communications ; they requiring a higher and more perfect condition than other and commonplace mediumistic writings.

Dr. Franklin, desiring to give me a series of papers for guidance and instruction, directed me to go to Boston in August, and remain in near proximity to Farnsworth, the medium, while there, which I did; and the following seven papers were given me, bearing date of each day that they were written. Several papers on scientific and philosophic subjects were given me during this time, which will be published in due season.

BOSTON, Aug. 15, 1863.

My Friend: — I am happy to be enabled to write and give you the information you so earnestly seek. I would not hold out to you the great benefit that you can be to your country, had I not thoroughly tested your mental power, the magnetic influence you are capable of exerting over persons, and the degree of influence that I hold over you in certain directions, when coming in direct contact with you, and by means of mediums also. I wish you to write to the members of the Cabinet. I will mention those whom I desire you to write to, as soon as conditions are ready for you to act in that direction. I will also give you forms of letters through this source, in the course of a few weeks; and here let me add, I shall without fail have this medium come to Chicago, so that he can be more available for you, and be directly under your influence and mine, so that I can do the greatest good by the use of his powers. The reason for not continuing these communications last January, was owing in part to counteracting influences working upon him, and some changes at Washington, that prevented my producing the change upon the officers there at the time I intended, but soon a broader avenue of action will be opened for me, and I shall bring about the desired result. I shall want you to write to some of the Governors of the various States.

At present I must withhold, for I wish to have the medium with you all the time, so as to give you the necessary instructions. It will take some time to carry out the plan that I have in view, and I must have conditions so that I can give you my sentiments. It will be but a few weeks before I shall want you to act, and I want you to keep the matter under consideration until that time, so that I shall find you fully prepared to proceed as desired.   Your Guardian,   *Franklin.*

Aug. 16, (A. M.,) 1863.

My Friend; — There is an electrical or magnetic mental atmosphere which pervades the entire universe, that emanates from mankind. There are also sympathetic poles or currents of nervauric influence passing through this magnetic atmosphere, (like telegraph wires in your atmosphere,) which establish relations between persons of a sympathetic and governing character. These vehicles of thought, or means through which the *will*, which is the great motive power of man, and upon which all the powers of the brain are dependent, is so subtile in its movement that at present it is not within the reach of man's comprehension to realize its action. It was many years after I left the earth before I was made conscious of this arrangement of the mental fluids — although while upon earth, electricity and its connection with ponderable agencies, was my highest pleasure to experiment upon.

This knowledge of the sympathetic relations between man that exists, and the power they possess of impressing each other at a great distance, and by exercise of the will control each other, first led me to the discovery of the possibility of spirit communion with the beings of earth.

There are sympathetic relations of the nature that I have described, existing between you and the Chief Magistrate of your nation, also with other leading officials; and with my aid, other conditions being favorable to impress the President and other persons, I am enabled to give you the plan by which your war must be settled — of which I have given you but an outline. Consequently the best mode for you to impress those persons, is to keep your mind and body in perfect health, and select certain hours of the day which will suit your convenience; desire with all your strength — appeal to the Fountain Head of power and justice, that you may have the desired effect upon the person you have in view.

Your writing to the person whom you wish to affect, will greatly facilitate the action of your nervauric influence upon him. The more vigor of will you possess, at the greater distance will you affect the party. The letter you wrote to the President last March, which I had knowledge of, was entirely satisfactory to me; it made a deep impression upon his mind, and has prepared him for further communications from you. Were it not for the opposition of his Council, he would have acted fully upon it; but he commenced to act in the direction that was given him, and has done all that in his power and province lay, to carry out the ideas that were presented to, and impressed upon him. The mode of operating upon the leading minds of your nation, I will endeavor to impart to you this afternoon. It is a matter that requires much attention, but I will assist you as much as possible.

The working of your mind upon persons is entirely unconscious to you, and it will be very difficult to make it so clear to you that you can fully realize the philosophy, but I can so advise you that you may increase your power over them. All natural laws are of themselves their own executors, working out their own possibilities. When a law is transgressed, the transgressor becomes a complete slave to that law — and must receive the just punishment.

The people of your country have taken from the negro the rights, the liberty that God has given him, consequently, from the natural working of all laws and principles, they must meet a just retribution.

I am known to both of your sons, and I think they will both communicate to you through this medium. Your son Joseph requested me to tell you that he would do so.

Your Guardian, *Franklin*.
Aug. 16, (P. M.,) 1863.

My Friend Richmond: — God is always and has ever been communicating with His children. This nervauric mode of communication is the most reliable, and it is by this system that I am now holding communion with you. These mental fluids are visible to me, also the established currents of sympathy existing between persons.

Concerning the relations that you hold with persons whom I have spoken to you of — I have tested the extent of your power which may be exerted over them. The writings of the ancient prophets, as those from me through this medium, are alike given.

There is a mental atmosphere arising from my spirit sphere, which is similar to your own, but more rarefied. Each spirit sphere has its mental atmosphere, and spirits existing in spheres above me, use similar modes of communication with me. The spirit world is connected by sympathetic relations, but of a more refined and higher character than the sympathetic relations of earth. As I progress, all matter is more refined and light is more brilliant. I arrive at your questions by communicating with your mind at the time I am writing. The use of the letter with the medium, is only to maintain the relations with you. The manner in which I get at your thoughts, is through the nervauric sense.

In communicating with you I endeavor to define items in the same manner in which you do, using your forms of expression — but in spirit life we count items in the order of things. There is much more I desire to communicate before you return home. I will write you again to-morrow morning. Your Guardian, *Franklin*.

Aug. 17, 1863.

My Friend: — I wish to speak to you at this time of your mission and usefulness. I have previously explained much to you concerning your present national difficulties. I have told you the cause of your civil war, and I have pointed out the only way by which you can have permanent peace, and justice rule supreme.

The negro race must declare its manhood. God asserts it, and as it has been abused by the people of the South, a just retribution must inevitably follow. *Negro soldiers will ultimate ·this war.* Not only will the South suffer from the hands of the unfortunate negro, but the people of the North, so far as they have been concerned in suppressing the freedom of the African, must receive their just punishment.

It is, then, demanded of you by a high power, to use all your efforts to impress upon leading minds the necessity of arming the negro in every possible way. I have already taken the initiatory steps towards this measure; through your means I have already affected the leading Magistrate of the nation, and as soon as I can make his advisers yield to the same impression, then I shall want you to take measures to have an interview with him, that I may exert a greater influence over his mind.

I am perfectly satisfied thus far as to the general effect that can be produced through your means upon the leading officers of your country.

Be not disheartened in laboring for justice and the elevation of the race; for in so doing you hasten your spiritual development.

Concerning all matters that you are not satisfied upon, I wish you to write and question me, as I am glad to communicate to you.

Your Guardian,   *Franklin*.
Aug. 18.

My Friend: — This mental atmosphere is of itself distinct from all other elements, and the currents of nervauric influence remain unmixed. By the laws of attraction and sympathy, these currents maintain a compact body, by virtue of their own system. These cords or magnetic poles are regulated by the action of your mind. The experiences you make mention of are the nervauric currents. I discovered the nervauric system of spirit communion with the beings of earth. Spirits have always communicated to earth, but in different forms.

God is always, and has ever been in communication with His children. The nervauric mode is the most reliable, and it is by this system that I am now holding communion with you. These mental fluids are visible to me, also the established currents existing between persons. Concerning the relation that you hold with persons, that I have spoken to you of, I have tested the extent of power which may be exerted over them.

The writings of the ancient prophets were the same as those from me through this medium.

There is a mental atmosphere arising from my spirit sphere which is similar to your mental atmosphere, but more refined; each sphere has its mental atmosphere, and spirits existing in spheres above me use similar modes of communication with me.

The spirit world is connected by sympathetic relations, but of more refined and higher character than the sympathetic relations of earth. As I progress, all matter is more refined, and light is more brilliant. * * * * The manner through which I get at your thoughts is through the nervauric sense.

Your son Joseph is progressing as fast as spirits usually do. His habits when upon earth were not formed through the promptings of his own nature, but from outside influences. Men only suffer from the wrongs they originate themselves. He is destined to become a bright and useful spirit.

    Your Guardian, *Franklin.*

August 19, 1863.

My Friend: — Your national government will not be so broken up as to destroy the value of its issues. The future government will not rest entirely on the basis of the old, but it will be reconstructed and new amendments adopted. But the government of the United States that is to be formed after the present crisis is passed, will be entirely of a new character, unlike any government now existing upon the earth. I will disclose its nature in due time. * * * *Franklin.*

On the 20th I wrote to Dr. Franklin that it was generally believed by the people of the North that the fighting was about done between the parties — that the *backbone of the war was broken.* I asked him if he did not so conceive it, presuming that he had a much clearer vision of the future than the people or myself had. He replied of same date as follows, in a note: " I do not consider that the ' backbone of the war is broken, ' as the feeling of oppression towards the negro race, both North and South, is not yet subdued. Apparently, your army has nearly conquered the South, but the end of this terrible strife is not yet. There must be a radical change in your political, social, and religious departments, and your people must be purified as by fire, before you can have permanent peace. Before the war is ended your army will consist largely of the negroes of the South, but much suffering will come to your people before this takes place.

" I tell you this as I receive it from the Source

of Justice, and I am commissioned by a high power to labor for the good of my country, that harmony may prevail, and the *true religion* be implanted in your hearts, that you may grow strong as a nation, and become in every sense of the term a progressive people."

These were Dr. Franklin's views. The "backbone of the war" was not in forts, stockades, arms, munitions of war, or troops of men, but in the *spirit* of the people, the feeling of oppression and injustice towards the negro. The South were guilty of the deepest injustice and oppression in making men property and beasts of burden.

The North was guilty of the crime of sustaining the South in its oppression, and of a deep seated and heartless prejudice against the negro. The "backbone of the war" lay in these crimes, in Dr. Franklin's view. Therefore the South must conquer its crimes, and the North its prejudice, before it was fully broken, and justice done.

As soon as the last message was given, I returned home to Chicago; the two following letters, bearing dates of 26th and 31st of August, came to hand in due time by mail. Early in September, the medium, Dr. Farnsworth, and his family, removed to Chicago. His condition after this was not always good; nevertheless he was used for short messages, sufficient for the purpose intended by Dr. Franklin.

BOSTON, Aug. 26, 1863.

My Friend: — I am happy to realize that the conditions for communicating with you are good, and I have a most perfect control of the medium.

The relations that I established during your last visit here, are permanent. At this time I think it best to give you the system of action that you are to carry out.

In the first place, when I deem it is best for you to write to the President and others holding important positions in your government, I shall give you the required instruction concerning the letters that you will write to them; and I wish you to think of what I have said respecting your national troubles, and with the assistance that I shall give you, by impressing your mind with the general plan, **frame for yourself letters to the President, and submit them to me.** I will then make the alterations necessary.

My reason for requesting this is that by this means I may prepare the recipient of your letters, so that I may have greater control over him; and by your giving attention to the matter, I can act with greater efficiency upon the sympathetic relations existing between you and the person to whom you are writing. I think it will not be necessary for you to place the letters you write, in the presence of the medium. I endeavor to make all of these matters plain to you, so that you may act with some degree of system.

After I have completed this matter, then I shall proceed to give the natural philosophy concerning many sciences, and a true religion which is necessary to the well being of human society.

I have the means at hand for carrying out these contemplations. Your present science of theology is based on *undemonstrable tales and evident misrepresentations*. Why not shape all your branches of knowledge upon systematic science? Why does society neglect the study of a rational religion — a religion compatible with human reason? I shall give you the knowledge of *natural theology* and *true morality;* also a correct system of society, by which all the beings of earth can be benefited, by association.

I shall want you to make the first move in this direction, after you have received the basis upon which to act upon the community.

Society at present is morbid in all of its relations, and is undergoing a change external as well as internal.

The people of earth are waking up to deep and earnest thought, and will receive and naturally adhere to progressive ideas; a great change is to take place in all your public institutions. The demand is made by the beings of earth, and it will be responded to by the Father of the universe.

Many good and powerful spirits have endeavored to establish societies upon a reform system on earth, but not having proper mediums and persons to act through, have partially failed; but they have performed their mission, and *now* I am instructed to act in the direction mentioned, and I have made selection of you to carry out my plans. I desire you to act in conjunction with me, and the world in which you live will be greatly benefited; your condition will be made higher, and of greater use to yourself and mankind.

Concerning this medium, I think it is best that he should go to your city as soon as he can reasonably prepare to leave here. * *

I thought it best not to give you a very lengthy letter this time — it being the first occasion upon which I have controlled him since you left.

Your Guardian, *Franklin*.

[Extract from Letter of Aug. 31, 1863.]

* * * I am with other spirits organizing electrical conditions in - Washington and other places, so that you will be better enabled to carry out that which will be given you to perform, and also that I can act with more power through you, upon the officers of your government.

Franklin

[Extract from Letter of Sept. 29, 1863.]

* * * In your letters to the President and others, I would like you to set forth the absolute necessity of arming all the negroes, and making use of all Southern resources that can be obtained, to defend the North and the right. You may begin the letter to the Chief Magistrate as soon as it suits your convenience, and I will review it before you send it to him. I wish you to write and forward all of the letters before the opening of the next Congress.

The next Congress which will assemble in the United States will be the most eventful one, and produce the greatest commotion in the nation, of any that has ever held counsel before. Great changes are soon to come to your nation, and from these changes the nation will emerge, purified and refined.

I am throwing influences about you and the medium, and developing you so that when the time comes for action, you will not be lacking in spiritual strength and capacity to do that which God desires of you. *Franklin.*

[Extract from Letter of Sept. 30, 1863.]
* * * Concerning the letters to the President and others, I wish you first to write a letter to the Chief Magistrate and then submit it to me for reviewal, after which it may be best to have it printed. I should like the letter prepared as soon as it meets your convenience.

Franklin.

If the familiar reader of Dr. Franklin's succinct and terse writings when in earth life, should take exceptions to what may appear to him tautalogy in these messages, he should consider the fact that the subject admits of little variety.

The grand object of the powers above was to abolish slavery, and to extend to the negro race its just rights. To accomplish this, everything was instrumental. To prepare persons for their positions as leading and active instruments was the first work. Mr. Lincoln must be elected as the chief official actor, because he was susceptible of Divine influences, and by means of other persons, could be made positive to those around.

I was appointed an instrument to act on Mr. Lincoln, as a force, a battery, and upon other officials because I was negative to the Divine, and positive to the world's influence, when coming in competition.

These messages came to me, for a period of ten consecutive years, to fit me and charge my mind with both the object and the work to be done by me. Subjects were often repeated of necessity. I must be instructed from time to time what to do. I must understand my use and mission. I must comprehend each message as it came, or ask of Dr. Franklin by letter, an explanation. His replies would come in language similar to the first given.

Again, long previous to any required action on my part, Dr. Franklin thought it essential to advise me of the work, and direct my mind to it, and he repeated it often, to more effectually prepare me for it. The continuous presentation of a subject was the means of preparing my mind for the use intended; spirits can much easier guide, quicken and enlarge a thought in a medium, than they can generate one.

In point of tautalogy or repetition, I think these messages will compare favorably with Moses' account of the emancipation of the Hebrew slaves from Egyptian bondage.

[Extract from Letter of Oct. 6, 1863.]

* * * Concerning the letter to the President, I know something of what you have written.

As soon as conditions favor it, I will endeavor to give you some thoughts concerning that epistle.

At present the spirits are holding congress. Spirits from different nations have met in council, and as soon as I am permitted, I will counsel you upon this matter. You have already accomplished sufficient to agitate the subject, and now you can drop it for a short time — and when it is best for you to act in the matter, I will inform you.

As at the present time you need assistance in your business, possibly it would be well for you to confine your thoughts to that direction, and it will give me a better opportunity to give you the aid you require of me.

Consider that in all of my communications to you, and the advice that I give you through this medium, I am compelled to use your mind as an agent, and in that way I can convey to you my thoughts, wholly separate from any influence; you thus receive my original thoughts. I speak of this, as I wish to make you acquainted with the conditions, so that you can give me more assistance. * * I can answer your questions when the medium is at any distance from you.

Franklin.

Dr. Franklin, having directed me to write to some of the Governors of the States upon the subject of the war, I did so, inditing letters to several of them. I did not retain copies, as at that time I had not learned that it was his design to have either his messages to me, or anything in regard to the war, published. The following is a copy of my letter to Gov. Todd, of Ohio, the only one I chanced to copy. Other letters were of similar import

CHICAGO, Oct 20, 1863.
GOV. DAVID TODD, OHIO —

My Dear Sir: As you now enjoy political position and power, consequently, have influence with the Administration and the war department of this nation, I presume to address to you a few thoughts, which I feel are pertinent to the hour, and condition of our country.

No rational man can doubt that slavery is the cause of the war now existing, nor believe that it will cease, so long as that cause exists

No one can doubt that the wisdom and power which organized this universe, intends this civil strife to culminate in the total freedom of the slave.

If this is a truth, it is wise for this government to act in perfect harmony with the higher Wisdom, and run its action parallel with those supreme designs.

Congress has adopted measures and enacted laws, giving varied and abundant powers to the Administration to confiscate rebel property, to enlist and arm the negro, and call out a large and formidable army from the African race. Abundant power and authority are given to the war department, to damage the enemy.

The President has issued his proclamation, setting free certain slaves, and has authorized the

the enroling and arming of negroes. So far, all is well done.

But, Sir, the *spirit* of these laws, and the proclamation, have not been felt nor carried out, by the various parties whose duty it has been to carry them into fullest execution.

Very little has been done under the confiscation law, compared with what should have been. A few negroes have been enrolled, armed, and brought into service, but there should have been ten where there is one. The fact is, a large portion of the officers in command of military posts, stations and districts, have entirely disregarded their duty in this respect, while others have but imperfectly fulfilled theirs.

General Rosecrans, several months in the heart of the rebellion, in the thickest of slavery, ought to have had sixty or a hundred thousand negro troops enrolled, armed and disciplined, with which he might have marched and conquered, with the aid of his own white troops, all opposing forces. Instead of this, he suffered defeat, shame, and reproach, and the loss of thousands of valuable lives, without having a regiment, company, or negro under arms.

Gen. Mead's army, in the heart of Virginia, has not, as far as I can learn, a negro regiment in it, notwithstanding the laws, the proclamation, and the hopes of the people.

Sir, there is a deplorable lack of spirit and loyalty to the laws of Congress, and the proclamation of the President, on the part of those in command, who are placed to execute them. The spirit of the laws and measures designed as instruments to conquer the rebels, does not exist sufficiently strong in the officers of the army, and of the government.

Three hundred thousand more soldiers are wanted; the States are called on, each to furnish its quota. With all possible fidelity and loyalty to the government, each State should respond to the call; but while you are urging volunteers to come forward and peril their lives in the service, you should *demand* of the President that *he at once* takes measures to fill the depleted ranks of the army with negro troops. Had there been efficiency in enrolling negro soldiers in time, the conscription would not have been necessary in July last, or the call now.

Our government must begin in earnest to damage the rebels and the rebel States.

First, and most effectually to do this, is to confiscate the able-bodied slaves, arm them, and make them an element of strength to us, at the same time taking the same element of power from them. Nothing would so distress and weaken rebellion, as to see its property, its slaves, in our army, ready to cut their way to freedom.

Why should we not immediately raise an army of half a million colored men and place them in the field, thus relieving Northern soldiers to till the soil, and continue their mechanical pursuits?

Why not save the lives and limbs of Northern men, and prosecute the war by the use of the physical force of those who have been the innocent and unconscious cause of it.

Sir, I venture the prophecy that a negro army will ultimate this war, and why not *now* commence in earnest to substitute the black for the white soldier?

Arm the negroes — promise them freedom! Give them the watchword and rallying cry of Liberty, Justice, Manhood! Give them good officers —those who are inspired by the *spirit of crushing out the rebellion with bullets*, and let them fight upon their native soil, to conquer their enemies and free themselves.

I beg of you, Sir, to use your influence, which is not small, with the President and heads of departments, to bring about this result.

I am very truly yours,
Thomas Richmond.
Nov. 12, 1863.

My Friend:—Again it gives me pleasure to communicate to you; conditions will soon be so that I can give you long letters. It is my wish that you should write to the President at your earliest convenience.

Your first letter to him served as a preparatory one for further correspondence with him. You will set forth in your letter that you are prompted to write to him by an invisible power, and that your own reason impels you. Advise him to have all the negroes in the State of Kentucky that can be influenced to join his army, as many of the people in that State will assist him to carry out this plan; also set forth to him the importance of raising as many negro soldiers as are possible — as they will be required in order to subdue every rebel.

You can copy the letter that you have already prepared, and embrace what I have given, and send it to him. My reason for not giving you a full letter and having you copy and send it to him, is, that it would not produce so good an effect as coming from your own mind — as that is used directly upon the will of the President, to influence him as we wish.

It will be my pleasure to write you concerning your personal matters, and after these matters are disposed of, I shall then give you letters upon scientific subjects. All my plans are working well. I shall endeavor to communicate to you briefly, daily, until conditions will allow me to communicate to you at length. Your Guardian,

Franklin.

[Extract from Letter of Nov. 13, 1863.]

* * * You can send your letter to the President by mail, and I think it will reach him. Write "private" on one corner of the envelope, and I will see that he receives it. Your letter of last winter reached him, and it had the desired effect upon him. Since then he has pursued the plan in part which that letter contained.

The plan set forth in that letter was taken into consideration by his Cabinet, and they partly acted upon it. I shall have a greater influence over him at the coming session of Congress. It is my intention that you hold direct communication with the President.

Facilities will be opened so that he may correspond with you. The present steps taken are a preparatory opening for future operations. I shall wish you to write to others besides the President. I will direct you at the proper time. I am arranging it so that your spirit children will communicate with their mother through this medium. *Franklin.*

Dr. Franklin usually impressed my mind with a subject, before writing to me upon it, and often urged me to act promptly upon the impressions as I received them, which I usually did upon familiar and important subjects. Nevertheless, it was not always clear that to my mind the impressions which I received were not the workings of my own spirit in whole or in part, and therefore I sometimes followed them hesitatingly. He always perceived the workings of my thought, and wrote to me through the hand of the medium, directing, correcting, or confirming my impressions.

In the case of the following letter to President Lincoln, I had, under impression, drawn up a skeleton of a letter, which I had laid by, being the one which he referred to under date of 12th, which I then finished and mailed, marked "private," as he directed in his last letter.

Chicago, Nov. 15, 1863.

ABRAHAM LINCOLN, PRESIDENT —

Dear Sir: I feel impelled by some invisible power, and my own reason responds to the influence, to write you.

Considering your valuable time and pressure of business, I will aim to be brief.

"Righteousness exalteth a nation, but sin is a reproach to any people."

This nation has been exalted just in proportion to its righteous dealing. It is now suffering reproach for the sins it has committed against the rights of humanity, in making beasts of burden and merchandise of men.

God intends that slavery shall cease, and the negro enjoy the rights which belong to humanity.

God has a way His own wisdom contrives. Cause and effect run together in all His works. Slavery has been the *cause* of our national strife, and this civil war is to be the *cause of the liberation of the slave;* but Sir, the negro must become an important element in attaining his own freedom, as the Hebrews were in gaining their freedom from Egyptian bondage.

Congress has done nobly in enacting laws and giving power to successfully prosecute the war. You, Sir, have done nobly in your proclamation of freedom to slaves in certain conditions, and in protecting and rewarding those who came into our lines. Still, the spirit of the laws of Congress and of the proclamation of freedom has not pervaded the war department — the army command. General Rosecrans, in the midst of slavery and rebellion several months the past season, had not a regiment, a company, or a negro armed and in battle, when he was forced to retire to Chattanooga. He might have had fifty to a hundred thousand armed and disciplined, enough to have marched through and conquered all the South, if he had possessed the will and spirit — but for lack of these he was forced to retire in disgrace before the rebel army.

Gen. Meade's army, in the heart of old Virginia some three years, has very few, if indeed any, regularly organized negro troops. It has had six different commanders and a few doubtful successes. This army should have had a hundred thousand negro troops well armed and drilled for service. Had these commanders possessed the spirit requisite to subdue the rebellion, there would have been a negro force sufficient to drive Gen. Lee with all his troops, from out the valley.

Sir, *the time has come when the North must feel more the spirit of damaging, and thus subduing, the rebellious States.* To damage them most is to take their property in slaves, which is and has been their support, and make them elements of power against them. To take away their strength and add to ours, is like taking out of one scale and putting it into the opposite one. There is nothing that can be done that would so dishearten the rebels, as to enlist, arm, and drill three or four hundred thousand of their negro slaves. There is nothing within the power of the Administration that would so soon bring this unholy strife to a close.

A million of Northern soldiers marching South would not, be so destructive to the hopes of the rebels as an army of half a million of negroes grown upon their own soil, with the watchword of Freedom, Justice, and Equality to the African race.

The North has poured out its treasures by millions, and given of its sons by hundreds of thousands. Thousands upon thousands have fallen on the battlefield, and thousands by disease, while nothing has been done by the four millions of people, who are the innocent cause of the war, but are to reap the benefit of it — their freedom.

It is hard keeping the army full by volunteers. Conscription is reprobated by many, yet a sufficient force *must* be had to subdue the rebellion.

As a motive to a man to enlist you offer four hundred dollars bounty, and thirteen dollars per month pay. Why not send recruiting officers into Kentucky and enlist every negro you can? The bounty you pay white men will *buy* the negro, if need be, and the wages will pay for his services; why not do so in every State? Thus the money that it costs to get a white recruit, would buy the negro, make him a soldier and freeman; aye, more than this would accrue from it. You would save the Northern farmer and mechanic to their friends and families, and make them producers rather than consumers.

You have already proclaimed liberty to the slaves in the Confederacy. Why not enlist, arm, and discipline them to the fullest extent, and *let them fight the battles of freedom for themselves?*

Why not compel the officers in command at all posts in the Confederate States to secure and arm every negro possible — and hereafter make up the depletions of the army from the ranks of the slaves, the property of the South?

Permit me, Sir, to urge the most hasty and extensive enrolment, arming and disciplining, a body of negroes in the South, and let that robbed, despised class share the peril, the labor and fame, of obtaining its freedom. Let them fight for it as our forefathers did for theirs, and our brothers do at this time.

A negro army is to ultimate this war, and the sooner that army is organized, the sooner will the sun of peace again shine upon this nation.

It is due the loyal North, which has done so *much*, to relieve her sons of the peril and labor of the army. It is due to the rebellious States to confiscate their property, and especially their slaves, and make a power of them to conquer their owners.

It is due to justice thus to damage the slave-holding rebels, and uplift the chattel negro. *It is due to the negro race to permit it to take an active part in securing its own rights, its freedom, and itself.* Sir, your boldest acts as Executive have been most approved; your Proclamation secured half a million votes this fall to the Union cause. Bring speedily an army of half a million negroes into the field, and thus relieve the Northern freeman to that extent from the army, and it will secure to the Union cause another half a million votes; and whether you seek or desire fame or not, it will give you a renown that will live as long as the nation lasts.

Sir, we have come to the swivel in the chain of our national life. Henceforth we are not to run in the track of the past. A new life begins here. A new history begins here; the future is to be erected upon this present.

A national life of justice is to be born out of this strife, and by "justice" this nation is to be exalted. *We must have no more national sins to reproach us. "Let the dead bury their dead," but we must hereafter follow justice.*

The true and real tree of liberty is now to be planted. The doings of this day, this hour, are going into history, into precedents. Future years will make a record of these.

Future generations are to come, and live, and read our doings, taking life and impulse of the spirit of this hour. God grant us a true national life of Right, Justice and Peace.

I am Yours Truly,
Thomas Richmond.
Nov. 18, 1863.

My Friend: — I was with you at the time you wrote the letter to the President. It was an improvement upon the rough draft you had prepared, and is satisfactory to me.

The manner in which I operate upon the President, is by using you as a means; first, by appealing to his reason through your writing to him; secondly, by using your magnetic system in conjunction with his, and thus establishing a sympathetic relation between the two. By means of these electrical and chemical relations I establish spiritual magnetic action upon his being. Even though he may be unconscious of it at the time that I am influencing him, yet the effect has a deep hold upon his nature, and as soon as I can make his surroundings spiritualized, and act in obedience to his interior, then I possess supreme control of his mental and physical being. *Franklin.*

[Extract from Letter of Nov. 20, 1863.]

* * * The use of the "circle of three" at Mr. Parmalee's in Boston, was to gather mental influences, to enable me to use this medium for the purposes that I have, and also to carry out and aid me in reaching the mind of the President and others who hold high positions in your national administration. *The " circle " served my purpose well*, and by its means I have accomplished all that I first contemplated. The explanation which was given you through Mrs. Parmalee at the time of the commencement of the circle, was nearly the same that I now give, but the influences were somewhat mixed, although I disclosed the object at the time. *Franklin.*

[Extract from Letter of Nov. 26, 1863.]
* * * Concerning your national affairs, I can only say that it will be difficult for me at this time to describe to you the course of the rebellion. It will be some time before you have peace, and many important changes will take place in the national affairs this coming winter.

Franklin.

[Extract from Letter of Nov. 27, 1863.]
* * * The President has read your letter but has had but little time to reflect upon it. He will give it his attention soon, and you will be directed to write him again in the course of time. I cannot say now as it will be necessary for you to visit Washington this winter. You will be advised about the matter. *Franklin.*

Nov. 30, 1863

My Friend: — I am with you in the morning, and occasionally in the evening. I come to you for the purpose of impressing you, and to unfold your spiritual powers, and operate upon your surroundings and magnetic condition, so as to penetrate your interior nature; it will be but a short time before you will perceive the light that will illume your being. Should you desire me at any time to come to you, and the influences permit me, I will be with you in a moment.

Some spirits are with you always. Spirits perceive no change in the condition of light, between night and day. Spirits that are highly progressed require but little rest. However, as a general condition in the spirit world, all spirits have a season for rest. Our nourishment is inhaled from the atmosphere as our natures require. We do not experience the desire for food that you do on earth, unless, it is spirits who are not progressed. Spirits cannot approach every person, consequently all have not guardian spirits.

The guardian spirits of the members of your family are familiar with certain matters, but not with all topics, as they are not all subject to the same influences, nor are they all on the same plane of developement. The guardian spirits of your household disagree in proportion to the disagreement of your family. The guardians sympathize with your spirits. Not all the persons in the form are subject to spirit influence, as some are so low in their natures that spirits cannot approach them. In proportion to your desires, cultivation, goodness, and mental capacity, so do you attract spirits towards you.

I know something of your correspondence with Mrs. A. I think your views upon the subject you spoke of, are correct. Mortals are subject to spirit control to the extent of their mediumistic capacity. In proportion to the spiritual unfolding of the beings of earth, do we control the earth—but the responsibility belongs principally to your atmosphere. We do not measure time as you do We have no fall, no winter; all is summer with us, and the fragrance of flowers is more exquisite than upon earth. It is every day with us, and the light that illumines the spirit world is far more brilliant than the light of earth. The sun and the moon are not visible objects to the spirit world.

Spirits can so influence your system in general, that you will not feel the effect of old age, as you would were you not subject to spirit influence.

    Your Guardian,   *Franklin.*

CHAPTER XIII.

From this last date until June, 1864, I received no direct communication in writing through the hand of the medium, from Dr. Franklin, on the subject of the war. During this time he had governed my movements in relation to the war entirely by impressions made upon my mind, still continuing to use my brain as a battery upon the officers of our national government. I was all this time subject to the impressions I received from that source in respect to national matters. Notwithstanding this, I was constantly corresponding with Dr. Franklin upon other matters, during this entire period.

Meanwhile, the medium was engaged in answering sealed letters for the public generally. By thus coming under the influence of promiscuous spirits, in answering their friends' letters, he became partially disqualified for the *precise* writings of Dr. Franklin upon the war or science.

When the preceding lengthy communications were written me, all other influences were excluded from the medium, Dr. Franklin keeping him under his own special influence.

From an extended communication upon other matters from Dr. Franklin, I give the following :

[Extract from Letter of June 19, 1864.]

* * * Governmental matters are going on as well as I could wish. The Chief Magistrate is becoming an instrument in our hands. Through your means I have gained much power over him, although the manner in which it has been accomplished may not be apparent to you.

* * * Consider that it is your organization that is the principal instrument used to bring about the greatest good in these affairs.

Franklin.

[Extract from Letter of July 13, 1864.]

* * * You are daily becoming more subject to spirit control. You were impressed to write to the President, and it is my desire that the letter be finished and sent to him. I would have you make an effort to assist the poor, as you will soon experience most distressing times. The people of the Northern States have great suffering to endure — it cannot be avoided. I predicted to you some time since the suffering that the American people must endure, in order to have a better state of things. You are now on the eve of this great event.

You will soon be brought into action. You are strong in yourself, and you have powerful aid from the spirit world. God is at the helm, and you are an important instrument to be used in carrying the nation through this trying period.

Wheat and flour will continue to advance in price, as well as other kinds of food. I see no danger yet in government securities. I think that Richmond must soon surrender. I cannot give you the exact date. *Franklin.*

CHICAGO, July 4, 1864.

ABRAHAM LINCOLN, PRESIDENT —

Dear Sir: I feel constrained by some irresistible power to again address you upon the subject of our national condition, and to make a few suggestions.

Causes, which always produce their natural effects, have been in operation, and worked out their legitimate results. The necessaries of life have advanced to such an extent as to place them beyond the reach of a very large portion of the poor in our land.

Until within a few weeks, breadstuffs have remained at reasonable prices, but are now nearly double the price of six months ago.

Not only is a terrible suffering of the poor at hand, but there is an enormous increase of the cost of carrying on the war. All the munitions of war and the necessaries of life have advanced to fully double their cost at the commencement of the rebellion, and there is now as great a tendency upward as at any previous time. The army needs men, and a call for a large number is at hand. The productive resources of the country are diminishing by reason of so much of the producing labor being called to arms.

Great consumption and waste is made by the army; besides, there is much labor drawn from the fields, to keep this army full — thus, many producers are made consumers thereby.

Now, Sir, what is to be done? Our gold is going out of the country with great rapidity, to pay, mostly, for needless merchandise, so we have none or little to spare to import the necessaries of life. This year's crop in the loyal States promises but very indifferently.

To go on, Sir, as we *have gone* with our army, until success comes, will cause distress at home, and create a national debt that we shall be hardly able to bear.

Again I ask, what shall be done? Shall we abandon the war, count ourselves too weak to subdue the rebels? No, I answer, no! *Prosecute the war with greatly increased vigor, and all the energy possible.*

We want more fighting men in the field. We must have more — but we should not spare them from the workshops and fields of the North. Taking the 100,000 laborers from our fields for one hundred days just in seeding time last spring, will tell fearfully upon the productions of the country, and the cost of the necessaries of life.

It appears to me, that were there a disposition among the commanders of the army, our supply of men might be kept up by the enlistment of negroes. I beg you to *make this a speciality in every department of the army, and everywhere in the slave States, rebel or not, where there are troops to protect them. Place officers friendly to the idea to enlist, organize and drill the blacks, and relieve our present army as fast as possible, by substituting the colored for the white soldier.* With a *will* and an *energy* on the part of the army officers, there can be no difficulty in raising a formidable army of colored men, and thus relieving our Northern troops to again enter into the producing department of this national service.

These are my views of what should be done, and that, too, with great promptness.

I beg, Sir, that you will consider that most important demands for the necessaries of life are at hand, and nothing but more producing labor can supply them.

Experience has proved the negro a good soldier — that regiments and divisions can be relied on in every emergency.

An election is approaching. Nothing would be more popular or profitable than to give special attention and make special effort to fill our depleting ranks with negroes, as fast as possible, and thus relieve our white soldiers, and permit them to return to their fields and workshops.

God and angels favor our cause, but they can only do it in the line of wisdom and justice. Do we ask Divine aid? Then let us as a nation and people, place ourselves in such a condition that

God can aid us, without patronizing inertia, folly, or wrong doing.

When we ask wisdom from God, let us walk in wisdom's ways, and when we implore success, let us use the means He has given us, *wisely, justly, and vigorously.*

Sir, I have barely touched upon leading points, to call your attention to them, and will not occupy your time with arguments.

I am Most Truly Yours,
Thomas Richmond.

HARMONIA, Aug. 4, 1864.

THOMAS RICHMOND — *My Friend:* I am by cords of attraction drawn to you. I come to strengthen and give to you more light upon this subject of spirit communion. Stand up before the enemies of truth, hurl defiance at them, bid them come on and draw their weapons, and see whose is the better tempered. Tell them yours is the blade of truth — *truth* forged in heaven, and that there is not a weapon carried upon this earth which can turn its keen and strong edge. So you shall find, my friend, if you stand before the world and draw this weapon, and let your banner float on the breeze, though all the world advance to crush you where you stand, they will melt away before you like the snow in the spring morn, leaving your pathway clear and pleasant to travel in.

Such is the power of real, heaven-born truth! The time has come when you should present yourself and the truths that you have obtained, to the world, and claim the consideration which is your due. I shall be glad to communicate with you further. At this time I can say no more.

Your Friend,
Daniel Webster.

HARMONIA, Aug. 4, 1864.

My Friend: — Seek to obtain a high elevation of thought, for as thou dost plant on earth, so wilt **thou seek** in spirit life the fruits of thy labor. Seek, **and ye** shall find within God's eternal presence the consummation of your perfected hopes; around thee will circle the radiant light emanating from the Divine, and reflected from thy crown unto the boundary of the universe. **Every angelic spirit** will know thee, and buds, blossoms, **and flowers will hail** thee as the one who sought the high and holy spheres of the spirit world.

Thy Friend,   *Wm. Penn.*

The two foregoing letters came spontaneously, without any movement on my part to influence them. They are very similar to the character of the writers. The first is in the strong, powerful language of Daniel Webster's stirring and arousing force. The latter partakes of the tender, paternal, careful, and advisory nature, peculiar to William Penn on earth. Both of them were of my circle of spirits.

My mother, who **had been** in the spirit world nearly sixty years, wrote me a long letter upon spirit life, through the hand of Dr. Farnsworth, **giving** me much practical information regarding that life, its employments and enjoyments. She gave me the names of some of my spirit circle and guardians; among them, she named Patrick Henry, of Virginia, of Revolutionary fame. Always having admired him as a man, a patriot, and being charmed with the inspirations of freedom and patriotism that fired his spirit and brain in the pivotal hour of the American Revolution, I felt that I wanted to speak to him and realize his spirit influence.

To effect this, I wrote to him about as follows:

CHICAGO, Nov. 20, 1864.

PATRICK HENRY —

My Dear Friend: My angel mother informs me that you are one of my guardian spirits watching over me, and using me in the management of our national government.

The great respect I always had for you induced me to write you, on learning that you were so near to me. I am studying God's works, Nature's works and laws, and *myself*. I see the natural man plainly enough, although I know but little of his external anatomy. I desire most to learn the anatomy of the soul — all its powers, faculties and functions. Can you teach me?

Yours Very Truly,
Thomas Richmond.

He replied to my inquiry through the hand of the medium, Dr. Farnsworth, on the same day, as follows:

THOMAS RICHMOND — *Sir*: I am one of your circle of spirits who are endeavoring to bring about a specific work, and you seem to be an instrument in our charge.

The anatomy of the soul and its functions is a profound subject, and in time you shall receive knowledge relating to it.

All power emanates from the brain; it is the center of power and health. All the organs of the brain must be active and perform their functions, in order that the individual may carry out God's intention and be healthy. Disease has its origin in the brain. You shall hear from me at length in good time.   Your Friend,

P. Henry.

In a lengthy communication upon various topics received on the 29th of August, 1864, Dr. Franklin writes the following upon governmental affairs:

My Friend: — I think government bonds are safe; at least, more so than your currency — (the promiscuous issues of the banks acting under State laws.) I think Lincoln will be re-elected. There is danger of physical strife at Chicago, yet it may not occur.

The result of your present war will be to liberalize humanity, and make it more truly progressive, and be the means of establishing a new religion upon earth, and bringing its beings nearer to God and His laws. The old will be done away, a new temple will be erected that will reach to the gates of heaven.   *   *   *   *Franklin.*

The communication from which the above was extracted, was written during the session of the Democratic convention in this city. Persons residing in Chicago at the time will remember the great peril we were in, and the deep apprehension of the people touching the presence of so many rebels. The part referring to government bonds, and the re-election of Mr. Lincoln, was in reply to my letter of inquiry to him on these points. The rest of it was written by his own prompting.

This letter was indited at Battle Creek, Michigan, and sent to me by mail, the medium then being at that place.

Nov. 6, 1864.

My Friend: — There is much excitement in the world around you, and I fear an outbreak in your midst, which will cause much suffering. I think it prudent for you to fortify yourself against any uprising of the people, or of the rebels who are now numerous in your city. I will be more definite with you as soon as the excitement is allayed, and other matters adjusted. *Franklin*

[Extract from Letter of Nov. 11, 1864.]

* * * There is yet much excitement in the political world, and I fear an outbreak.

We are now giving the most of our attention to national matters. We shall give you our instructions when conditions are all prepared. It is best that you read matters of a general character only, to the family. *Franklin.*

CHAPTER XIV.

From November up to the following date no written message came to me from Dr. Franklin, through the hand of the medium, upon the subject of the war.

There were no new measures to be pressed upon the administration. All that were designed by the Spirit Congress in the management of the war, had been given to the President, and urged with great force, repeatedly.

Congress had provided by law all necessary means for the present condition of things. The great necessity was to *carry into execution* the measures already presented to the administration. Dr. Franklin was able to impress my mind to do all that was necessary, while he was using it as a battery, as he has described, upon the executive department of the government, invigorating its action.

In the meantime the medium was doing an extensive and successful business answering sealed letters for all who sought correspondence with spirit friends, in which he generally gave great satisfaction, he residing in the family with myself.

Dr. Franklin could control the medium when near me, much better than elsewhere, and could impress me more forcibly when I was in his sphere; and consequently, at Franklin's express desire, we lived in the same family and condition during this period.

May 18, 1865.

My Friend: — Abraham Lincoln is with us. We had the knowledge that he would be assassinated. His mission upon earth was finished. He was prepared to make the change, and it was best and in order that he passed on to higher conditions. He recognizes your condition and relations to him, and the means used through you, to control him.

He desires to communicate with you. He came to Mrs. Lull, on the second day of his assassination, through your "circle of three." * * You are to hold an interesting correspondence with him, and also be the means of assisting his wife. Your Guardian, *Franklin.*

On receipt of the above communication I wrote to Mr. Lincoln, asking a number of questions touching his administration, and knowledge of influence from the spirit world, through myself and others, and received the following reply. This was about forty days after his death.

May 25, 1865.

My Friend: — I shall not be able at this time to answer your letter in detail. I did receive your letters while in Washington, and they exerted an influence upon me. I was governed much in the management of national affairs by direction from the spirit world.

I perceive *now* that you had a great influence upon me. As soon as I have more power to communicate, I shall be happy to, as I desire to say much to you. Your Friend,

A. Lincoln.

CHICAGO, Aug. 24, 1865.

ABRAHAM LINCOLN — *My Esteemed Friend:* Your favor of May 25th was duly received; you thought you would write at greater length at some future day.

Please tell me what influence was brought to bear upon you while President; explain as far as possible how it was done.

Were your thoughts drawn to me at all? Was it my influence upon you that induced the proclamation? Was it my influence that led to the measure of arming the negroes? Was mine the influence that prompted the removal from command of the officers who did not choose to fight? Were there other medium channels through which the congress of spirits influenced you?

Do you think that the rebel States will come in good faith into the Union, and co-operate with the North, and make a happy nation?

Are you aware of the "circle of three" *viz.*, myself, Mrs. P. and Mrs. L., organized in Boston, December, 1861, after your first election? Has

that "circle" been of any benefit to you during your life on earth?   Truly Yours,
Thomas Richmond.

BOSTON, Sept. 6, 1865.

My Friend: — I cannot at this time explain the manner in which our influence was brought to bear upon me through you, while I was President, but my thoughts were drawn to you, and upon the letters you sent me. By them I was led to the measure of arming the negroes, and the removal from command of officers that chose not to fight.

There were other channels through which I was influenced, but the governing influence came through you and your "circle."

In time the rebel States will come in good faith into the Union.

There is more that I would like to say, but cannot now. I will communicate soon again.

Truly Your Friend,
A. Lincoln.

Two days after Mr. Lincoln was assassinated, he came to Mrs. Lull, one of the "circle of three" above referred to, and was recognized by her, and talked with her. About forty days after his assassination he wrote me his first letter, and about four months from that time the above letter was written.

With so little experience and practice he could not hold the medium under control long, consequently these two letters were very brief. Near the close of this book a lengthy and very intelligent letter will be found.

The first American spirit acquaintance I made after resolving to investigate Spiritualism, was that of John Quincy Adams, known as the "Old Man Eloquent," ex-President; and for several months of my earliest investigation he was my teacher, as before related.

This early spiritual acquaintance led us into correspondence through Mr. Farnsworth, the medium, as well as Mr. Spear.

The two following items are notes appended to somewhat lengthy communications from Mr. Adams to me, and at the dates named. They are spontaneous expressions of his thought.

[Extract from Letter of Aug. 19, 1865.]

* * * You have already served an important mission to your country by giving spiritual assistance to Mr. Lincoln, as spirits through you controlled him as they desired. He is now conscious of your real position, and in him you have a strong spirit friend, who will afford you much comfort.

Your Friend and Guardian,
J. Q. Adams.

[Extract from Letter of Sept. 27, 1865.]

* * * You are not used directly to act upon the President as formerly, but Lincoln through you, still has an influence in the government.

We wish franchise extended to the negro, but the time has not quite come for women to have the right extended to them. Your Guardian,
J. Q. Adams.

CHAPTER XV.

In the years 1865-6, I had few written communications from Dr. Franklin through the appointed medium, upon the subject of our national matters. Several reasons existed why he did not communicate as formerly.

First, the medium was seldom in proper condition for control and use; second, the rebels had been subdued. Mr. Lincoln had been assassinated, and there were no active measures going on during this period. My brain, however, was open to impressions to the extent of Dr. Franklin's desire to communicate.

Early in November, 1865, I had a violent attack of erysipelas, and my life was barely saved. This illness controlled my physical movements until the May following, during which time I was mostly confined within doors.

This was my condition during the sitting of the Congress of the winter of '65-6, the first session after the rebels were subdued, and had laid down their arms.

During this session of Congress the work of reconstruction was agitated. Many plans and projects were suggested. Much argument and debate was held in both Houses; bills were introduced and resolutions offered. The matter was thoroughly agitated and canvassed, but no definite settlement of principle or conditions of the return of the rebel States to the Union, was agreed upon.

Dr. Franklin required me in my sick room to keep well informed on all public matters, and especially to be posted with regard to each day's doings in Congress, which I did, to the best of my opportunity. Being physically much exhausted, and having no business on my mind, my brain was very impressible, and I was somewhat clairvoyant, so that Dr. Franklin was able to impress me to do things without resorting to the medium. Thus, my directions came through my own organism principally. He had all along urged me to trust my own impressions, as he preferred to come direct to my own brain and understanding, as far as possible, rather than to use a medium's.

From day to day, as I read the action of the administration or the Congress, Dr. Franklin would say to me, write to this or that person, point out the error of that plan, sentiment, or principle; or he would direct me to encourage and strengthen this one or that, as the case might be, always giving me confidence that there were spirits to accompany the letter, and give it force and power upon the party written to. I felt assurance too, that Dr. Franklin would guide my mind to say the exact thing intended by the spirit congress, and felt no anxiety about the matter or style of my letters.

During that session of Congress I wrote numerous letters — amongst them I addressed the following persons: President Johnson, Senators Sumner, Wilson, Yates, Trumbull, Howe, Sherman, Fessenden; and of the House, Thaddeus Stevens, Bingham, and many others. Sumner, of the Senate, and Thaddeus Stevens, of the House, were the leading Radicals — the magnates of right and justice to the negro race.

These were all written by impression, and were, no doubt, instruments in the hands of spirits to prevent any reconstructive measures from being adopted at that session, or at any time, until, by these influences, the congressional mind had been made radical enough to pass in laws the radical and just measures that had been determined on and adopted by the spirit congress.

Dr. Franklin gave me assurance that there should be embraced in the general measures of restoration to the Union of the rebel States, perfect equality to *all* — the same right and justice to the black man as the white; and that no reconstructive measure should ever become a law that did not carry in its train the sublime principle of *equal and exact justice.* Nor did I fear or tremble, for *I knew that God had taken this American nation in hand*, and however wicked or corrupt individuals might be, *He would never permit a restoration and union of the States, until all distinctions as to rights were removed, and exact equality, freedom and justice to all should be secured and become a fixed principle in the Constitution and supreme law of our nation.* In the words of General Jackson, "God has had His own way." "He has made the people willing in the way of His power." The grand principles that have been forced through Congress were above the sentiment and principles of the individual members at this time. In some other part of the book I will show more fully the working power of the invisible world as manifested in producing these grand results.

The great work for which the rebellion was instituted is accomplished, but not the whole work of the nation in the distribution of justice.

There must be equal rights, equal freedom, and equal justice extended by our laws, to the mothers, the daughters and the sisters of the favored and enfranchised.

Why should this be denied or delayed; why not do it *now* and cheerfully, rather than linger and have it wrenched from us by long labor and protracted effort? God and the angel world are pledged to extend the freeman's right to the women of the land. The only question is *time.*

[Extract from Letter.]

* * * It will not be out of place for me to go back to your early experiences in spirit communion, as all that we have to say to you must appeal directly to your reason, and be given to you upon the plane of your comprehension, in

order to benefit you, or instil into your being the wisdom and power that is intended. Many years ago, before Spiritualism was thought of in the United States, you were selected by an assembly of spirits, for the specific object of establishing a change in society and organizations, which required reformation.

You were selected for this purpose because you possessed the elements of mind and body which could be acted upon by the spirit world to develop great reforms. I was the principal agent in producing the first manifestations to the people of America.

As soon as I entered spirit life, I found that I had been prepared during my experience upon earth, for my mission to open the channels of communication to the beings of earth.

You were selected, and since the selection conditions have been prepared for your development, and all has passed along in order, with the exception of some apparent failures, and even these disappointments have resulted in your good.

I wish you to consider that spirits in communicating have much to oppose, and that we cannot at all times do as we wish; but notwithstanding this opposition, there is a power behind all this, that accomplishes its first design, and if we but act up to the best conditions, these adverse influences will strengthen, illuminate and beautify the spirit, and make the mind more determined to surmount difficulties and accomplish the object.

We have found in you from the commencement the spirit of determination, and it has attracted towards you many wise and bright spirits, and every day of your existence develops powers within yourself, and these are continually forming guards around the external avenues of your being, to protect your spirit from the contaminating influences of earth life. * * Your action is the result of will, or of your concentrated thought; and to seek for knowledge in the right direction, would be to turn within yourself to the thoughts which cause your action. *Franklin.*

[Extract from Letter of Jan. 8, 1866.]

* * * What we ask of you is to aid us by exercising your judgment, and act in concert with us, in arranging external conditions.

Concerning the papers in relation to the late civil war that you have received, it is our design to have them published, and we would like to have you arrange them for publication. I think that Mr. Lincoln will be able to control this medium, and give you interesting papers to be added to them. Your Guardian,

Franklin.

The foregoing is an extract from a lengthy letter from Dr. Franklin, touching various subjects that had been a matter of correspondence between us, and which at some future day will be issued under its proper title. This suggestion of collecting the papers, and selecting the passages relating to the late civil war, from the numerous communications

I had received from spirits, was the **first** intimation I had received that he proposed publishing them.

Had this intention of **Dr. Franklin's** been known to me from the commencement, I should have kept a diary of events — made a record of transpiring things, and the impressions given me from time to time, which governed my action and sustained my faith, inducing my personal services and expenditures of money. I should have introduced a great number of deeply interesting and wonderful incidents, which now have too far escaped my mind for intelligent rehearsal. Doubtless, however, it is better as it is. The wisdom above has governed it in the light of the Divine Mind.

CHICAGO, Jan. 23, 1866.

My Friend: — Although I am not now connected with your spirit circle, I have knowledge of your "circle of three." It was formed through spirit promptings and influences, for the purpose of aiding in national affairs, Dr. Franklin, Adams and Washington, being the controlling spirits. Their motives were to produce influence through you, by means of the circle, upon President Lincoln and others high in office, to sustain them through the conflict, and to abolish slavery. All this has been accomplished, you being an important instrument in the hands of the spirit world to bring it about. Your letters to Lincoln had the desired effect upon him. I trust that you have a copy of the letters you wrote him.

My friend, it would give me much pleasure to speak in detail upon this important matter of your use as an instrument in the hands of the spirits controlling you, and also of national affairs, and the future destiny of your people, but the conditions of the medium will not permit me. I think, however, before you have the matter all arranged for publication, I shall be enabled to give you several papers. Your Spirit Friend,

Daniel Webster

Jan. 24, 1866

My Friend: — It is best that you have published all of the communications relating to the late war.

Others which you have received, that came from the congress of spirits, I do not deem best to have published with the war communications, but they are to be held in reserve for a future book. It would be my highest pleasure to give you a full communication relating to this late war, but at this time the medium is not in condition. Dr. Franklin is arranging matters so that he, myself, and other spirits, may communicate in full upon the subject through this medium, so that you may have more for publication.

Your Friend,

J. Q. Adams.

RANDOLPH, MASS., Feb· 7, 1866.

My Friend: — I have now arranged all the conditions so that the spirits whom you have requested to answer your letters may be enabled to control the medium. I hope in the course of a few days to have him in condition, so that Adams and other spirits will be enabled to communicate to you at length, that you may have their papers published in your book of the war.

Your Guardian, *Franklin.*

RANDOLPH, Feb. 9, 1866.

My Friend : — The following spirits, Napoleon, Joan of Arc, Josephine, Marie Stuart, and Andrew Jackson have all been present, and controlled the medium to their best ability. Of course, they could not say all they desired, but they think they have given sufficient to prove to you and others that they controlled Miss Barrett, and that the communications you have received, came from those spirits.

Owing to conditions not being wholly fit at the time when their communications were given you, due allowance must be made. The conditions to-day are not as good as need be, in order to transmit all that is desirable. Nevertheless all that you have received and will receive to-day, proceeds from the persons in spirit life whose signatures they bear.   Your Guardian,

Franklin.

The above paper and the one next previous, will show conclusively, that Dr. Franklin took charge of the medium and fitted him as well as the spirits using him for these communications, and that he superintended them. It is interesting to contemplate this movement. I addressed my letters of inquiry to the parties named. Dr. Franklin having ordered the papers on the war collected and published, and knowing that I had written those parties for these test answers, entered at once into the object of it, and being an expert in preparing mediums, and communicating with earth, fitted and prepared the parties for the work, saw it accomplished, and certified to it by letters. This is just like him.

CHICAGO, Jan. 25, 1866.

ANDREW JACKSON — *My Friend:* A letter written in August, 1862, through Miss Barrett, of Manchester, N. H., bearing your signature and in your style, reached me. I am now, by advice of Dr. Franklin, gathering such communications and extracts as have come to me from spirits, concerning the late civil war. Will you please write me what was the object and subject of that letter? My aim is to collect such a mass of testimony as will be convincing to the religious mind, that God brought about the civil war in this way in order to abolish slavery, and as a just retribution for the sins of the nation; that spirits under favorable circumstances do communicate with persons on earth; and that there is an active commerce going on between the two worlds.

I am Your Friend,
Tho. Richmond.

RANDOLPH, Feb. 8, 1866.

My Friend: — God brought about the late civil war. Justice demanded that American slavery should be forever abolished. Praises be to God

He has had His own way. It could only be brought about by the shedding of blood. You have served an important mission in the hands of God, in the affairs of your nation. I communicated to you at the time you refer to. It is not necessary for me to tell you your mission, or by whom you were appointed, as it has been given you from several sources.

The truth will sustain you. You are right.

Your Spirit Friend,
Andrew Jackson.

CHICAGO, Jan. 25, 1866.

My Dear Friend Josephine: — A short note reached me in August, 1862, bearing your signature, written through the hand of Miss Barrett, of New Hampshire. Did you write or prompt that letter; if so, state what was the occasion of it at that time, and why addressed to me.

If I had a mission to perform in regard to the subject of it, please state what it was, and by what authority I was appointed, and if I have thus far filled it. Dr. Franklin advises me to publish the communications from spirits, touching our recent civil war and my instrumentality in the premises. Please reply at your earliest convenience.

Sincerely Yours,
Tho. Richmond.

RANDOLPH, MASS., Feb. 9, 1866

My Good Friend: — I communicated to you at the time you refer, upon the subject of the war. My object was to inform you of your mission.

You were selected by a circle of spirits, whose names have already been given to you. You have fulfilled your mission nobly, and have been faithful to your charge. It would be my pleasure to say more, but I cannot further control the medium

Your Friend, *Josephine.*

CHICAGO, Jan. 25, 1866.

My Dear Friend Mary Stuart: — In August, 1862, nearly four years since, I received a short letter with your name attached, through the hand of Miss Barrett, of New Hampshire.

Will you please say whether you were the author of that letter, and what circumstances or condition prompted you to write it. Please state *why* it was addressed to me, and if any action was desired on my part by spirit friends, what mission I had, and by whom appointed. That note of 1862 and the one you write in reply to this, I shall publish. My object is to obtain matter for a book that shall appeal to the religious sentiments of the people. Your spirit presence has done me much good; I have felt great satisfaction in it, for which I thank you.

Your Appreciative Friend,

Richmond.

RANDOLPH, Feb. 9, 1866.

My Dear Friend: — I was the author of the letter through Miss Barrett. You were an important instrument in the hands of the spirit world, to bring about a great result for the good of your country. Through the action of your powers the

Chief Magistrate of your country was influenced to issue the Emancipation Proclamation, and to take other measures to benefit your people. You were appointed by the congress of spirits. I can say no more now. Your Friend,

Marie Stuart.

Marie Stuart is more generally known as Mary, Queen of Scots. I have known for many years that she has been a member of the circle of spirits who have had me in charge, and so has Josephine. Consequently, I felt quite well acquainted with them, and wrote somewhat familiarly.

I had written them before, and had correspondence with them on other subjects, and gained much instruction from them, touching spirit life. My correspondence with these lady spirits has been agreeable to both parties, and very instructive to me. I am their pupil—they are my teachers. It is both their duty and pleasure to instruct me, and all mortals whom they can approach, and who will receive and can appreciate their teachings and friendship.

CHICAGO, Jan. 25, 1866.

My Friend Napoleon: — In August, 1862, I received a paper bearing your signature, from the hand of Miss Barrett, of New Hampshire. I write you now simply to learn from you if you wrote it, and what was your object.

Yours Truly,
Richmond.

RANDOLPH, MASS., Feb. 9, 1866.

Sire : — I did communicate to you at the time to which you have reference. I am interested in the affairs of your country, and perceived that through your agency much good might result to your nation.   I am,   *Napoleon.*

CHICAGO, Jan. 25, 1866.

My Friend Joan of Arc : — Please write me if you impressed Miss Barrett in the summer of 1862 to write me. I am about to publish the communications that came to me on the subject of our civil war, from spirits who were interested in the success of our cause.   Truly Your Friend,

Richmond

RANDOLPH, MASS., Feb. 9, 1866.

My Dear Sire ; — I remember I communicated to you in the summer of 1862, through the medium to whom you refer.

My influence at the time was necessary to prompt you to action, you being a medium in the hands of the circle who had you in charge. You have fulfilled your mission to your country, and a great reward awaits you.

Your Friend,   *Joan of Arc.*

Some critics may find matter for carping in regard to the signature of this last message, "Joan of Arc." They will say that this is not her real name — that if she had written it, she would have signed her name correctly.

In reply to such criticism, I have to say that in correspondence with spirits, they reply in the terms and language we use to them. I addressed her "Joan of Arc" — she signs herself so in her reply. She is universally written so. I know that her name is Jeanne d'Arc. This mode not being in general use, I addressed her in the way most commonly known. She replies in the same style.

The following letter was written as dated, to President Johnson. At this time he had not fully determined his "policy," nor had his antagonism to Congress and the Republican party developed itself so fully as it did subsequently.

CHICAGO, Feb. 12, 1866.

ANDREW JOHNSON — *President:* I feel impressed to give you a few thoughts upon the unsettled condition of our governmental affairs. The crisis through which our country has recently passed, the wrongs, the injustice, which heretofore existed, and brought upon us this terrible calamity, should admonish us that wrong doing only produces evil. God cannot give permanent prosperity to a people that ignores justice in its fundamental law. Righteousness only can exalt a nation. As we are now about to re-establish a national union of States, we must avoid all former errors, and lay no unsound materials in the basic structure. Let Justice be the corner stone, Equality and Freedom be secured to every one. Consider, that what is one man's right before the law, is *every* man's right.

The spirits of justice, right and freedom are

living spirits, and *eternal;* any adjustment of the union of the States, that is not based upon these immortal principles, can only be temporary, like rotten wood in a foundation wall. For forty years the political elements of the country have been in commotion.

The spirits of Justice and Right have been struggling for recognition and acknowledgment in regard to the African race, nor could they be stayed by bargain or compromise, or any effort, until slavery, the "sum of all villanies," was removed. Nor can it be stayed *until every right that the white race enjoys is also extended to the colored. In all his rights before the law, and in all his privileges, the black man must be equal to the white man.*

Sir, heal up the wounded body politic — restore the union of the States, upon any principle save that of exact equality, and you only continue the cause of further strife between right and wrong.

In or about 1850 Congress "settled" the matter by a compromise between right and wrong, which only increased the strife by continuing the cause, which culminated in the late civil war. *Justice would not be sold out to slavery.*

Why not give the black man his rights at once? God demands it; the spirits of Right and Justice will fight for it until attained. Do right, and have peace; refuse, and have war and strife. Choose ye, between them!

The acts and doings of the Administration and

government are going into history, and this is an important hour. The world is taking note of the doings of the men in power of America.

I am Truly Yours,
Thomas Richmond.

* CHICAGO, Feb. 15, 1866.

HON. CHARLES SUMNER — *My Dear Sir:* I am pleased with your course, and your views as Senator, in regard to the adjustment policy. I fervently hope that you will *never modify your principle or plan, and never abate your effort*, until by constitution and law all adult humanity stands equal before the law.

Congress now seems to have the power to hold the rebel States at bay, until their constitution and laws give justice — the same privileges to the black as to the white population.

Respectfully Yours,
Thomas Richmond.

CHICAGO, Feb. 20, 1866.

HON. THADDEUS STEVENS — *My Friend:* Your sentiments are right, touching reconstruction; your idea is the highest and truest one. *You must maintain that position!* Maintain that the right of the negro is as precious as that of the white man. Never come down a whit from the lofty principle of *equal rights and justice* to the negro. Make him equal to the white man in all his rights, as far as law can make him so.

You, Sir, have taken this strong ground. I beg you to maintain it. I have confidence that you

can carry the most radical measures suggested. The people look to you as "a cloud by day, and a pillar of fire by night." Be positive, be strong, be firm.   Truly Yours,
Thomas Richmond.

On the 13th of April I wrote to Dr. Franklin, as follows:

My Friend Franklin: — I received your letters accompanying those of Bonaparte, Joan of Arc, Marie Stuart, Josephine, and Andrew Jackson, certifying them to be written by the parties whose names are signed thereto. At the same time that the above spirits wrote me, in 1862, and in the same package, a letter from Isaac T. Hopper came. A few weeks since I wrote to Mr. Hopper as I did the others, asking a verification of that letter. My letter was returned to me by the medium unanswered, together with those above, which were answered. Please inform me why Mr. Hopper did not reply to it?

I wrote to Mr. Lincoln, Gen. Washington, Jefferson, Adams, Webster and others, in one general letter. None of them have replied to me.

Why are not these letters answered? Is it on account of my weak and bad condition when I wrote the letter, or my subsequent feebleness? or was it because I addressed them all in one letter?
Yours Truly,   Thos. Richmond.
May 10, 1866.

My Friend: — We cannot communicate upon these important matters, unless we have the best conditions. You were not in good health when you wrote the letter, and the medium for months has not been in a fit condition for us to control him so that we could fully give our views upon national affairs; and we would not attempt to communicate unless we could say all that was desirable. I. T. Hopper has not communicated because he could not gain control of the medium. Conditions are being brought about with you and Mr. Farnsworth, so that we shall be enabled to give the papers necessary to complete your book upon the war.

The medium must not be controlled by other spirits while we are giving these communications, as it makes his condition too much mixed. As he has taken his notice from the public prints, and is going into the country, we think we shall soon be able to give you all the matter requisite for the war book and other purposes. We desire you to hold regular correspondence with him, so as to have him prepared for the work in question. You must be patient, and wait the result.

We are now using our influence at Washington through your mediumship. We wish you, Mrs. L., and the medium to be in perfect harmony, so that we may be able to use greater power for the good of your country. Your Guardian,

Franklin.

[Extract from Letter of May 10, 1866.]

The letter from which this is taken, was addressed to myself and another party.

* * * I am in hopes soon to have conditions with this medium, so that the communications upon the war can be given for the book. Mr. Richmond is being used by spirits to influence Congress. Of course we are agreed with him in his views concerning national affairs. I am much pleased with your arrangement. You can both be of great service to humanity, and you are now in good condition to be used by the spirits.

Mr. Farnsworth cannot be used as a medium in the manner that he has been for the past year, and I think it best to gring him to Chicago for a new phase of mediumship, and to be in connection with Mr. Richmond, when I shall try to give further communications for the war book.

Franklin.

BOSTON, Dec. 12, 1866.

My Friend:—The medium's conditions have been such that I could not communicate to you as formerly, although I still consider him the best channel of communication that I have, when I can get control of him without having other influences to operate against me. We continue to use you as an instrument for the good of your country, and it is in order and best that you should visit Washington this winter. It is not necessary for you to make a visit to Boston, but as it is best for you to take your wife to Vermont, you might stop a day or so there. I would like to have you call upon Mrs. Parmalee, and talk with her. In all probability the medium can make arrangements for you to stop in the house with him. As he has an invitation to go to Washington you had bettei take him with you. I wish you to come together, for I desire to complete my communications to you upon scientific subjects, and I want him with you when in Washington.

The object of your visit there will be made manifest when you arrive. The most favorable month for you to go there, is January. * * You do all that I desire of you.   *Franklin.*

CHAPTER XVI.

In the earliest notice that Dr. Franklin gave me of my duties, mission and use, he stated that at the close of the year I would be used in re-organizing and reconstructing the government.

The war having been brought to a close by the surrender of Richmond and the rebels, the next measure necessary was to reconstruct the national government. In accordance with this design I was instructed to go to Washington and attend the session of Congress for the winter of 1866–7, and to be there as early as January. In obedience to these instructions, I arrived in Washington on the 22d day of January, 1867, Mr. Farnsworth being with me. I reported myself to Dr. Franklin by addressing a note to him and handing it to the medium, stating that I was ready for instructions and service, also requesting him to call the attention of the spirit of Dr. Rush to the bruise that I had received.

On my way there I had bruised one of my limbs, and having had a very dangerous attack of erysipelas a short time before, arising from a similar bruise, I was much alarmed about it.

WASHINGTON, Jan. 23, 1867.

My Friend: — I am very happy to have the opportunity of communicating to you in this city. All the spirits who have been the leaders of your country are so yet, and are assembled here; and it is here that we can use your powers to the best advantage, for the benefit of the nation. We wish you to be in the House of Representatives and Senate Chamber as many hours each day as circumstances will allow, and mingle with the members, so that we may diffuse an influence through your organism, and thereby exert a power upon the entire Congress.

Make manifest to those you come in contact with, your impresssions. Speak plainly all the thoughts that will be given you.

This is a severe ordeal that the nation is passing through; you have been prepared for the work before you.

Let nothing change your course, as much depends upon you, and *you* will be held responsible. Concerning the medium and your boarding place, you have not the most favorable conditions for receiving the influences that we aim to impart to you both. It would be better for you to take your meals in a more quiet manner. To be alone while eating, would be the best condition for you, or to eat with persons whose belief and sympathies are congenial.

We do not like the atmospheres connected with your rooms. However, they will do until you have time to procure a better place. It is the intention of the circle to have you remain here some weeks, and possibly months. The length of time is not yet decided that the medium will remain, as he will be uneasy and unfit for writing unless he receives pecuniary support. We will endeavor to impress you both so that you may get rooms and board better suited to your condition. It is best that you and the medium sleep apart, and in separate rooms, if possible.

By sleeping together your magnetisms become too much assimilated, and neither of you will have the power to carry out that which you are capable of doing; you have separate spheres of action to operate in, and should take all methods to be in good condition. Consider that your mission to this city is for the good of the nation, and is to be the means of preventing greater disturbance in national affairs.

Follow your highest promptings. I will communicate each morning, but the medium cannot be controlled for other matters now. Write to me each day. Your Guardian,

Franklin.

Jan. 24, 1867.

My Friend:—The religious war is not as near at hand as you heard predicted last evening, through another medium. There will be a great conflict, but I do not apprehend any bloodshed. We hope to prevent that, although there is a tendency to another civil war—still, we think it can be prevented, if the men who now rule in Congress are faithful, and remain bold and firm in their resolution.

There can be no measures adopted which are *of too radical a nature!* The time has come for immediate and decisive action.

The tyrants of your nation must be subdued. There ccan be no ompromises, no leniency shown — the time for that is past.

High Heaven proclaims justice for the downtrodden, and we as messengers from higher courts are knocking at the doors of your Congress, proclaiming the will of our Chief, *and it must be obeyed! You, with all other instruments who have been chosen and prepared for this great crisis, must be firm.*

Be faithful, remain at your posts. Let God use you for the good of the nation, and your reward will be great. * * * Dean Richmond is very desirous to communicate with you, and will soon. You can assist him much.

Your Guardian, *Franklin.*
Jan. 25, 1867.

My Friend : —You have been directed to come here by high influences, and will not be permitted to leave until your mission is performed; by keeping you here, if you understand and follow our directions, you will not be embarrassed, but the way will be made clear for you.

We want you to be upon the floor of the House of Representatives when you visit the capitol;

but for a few days follow your impressions and inclinations, as to when you should make the visit to the House.

Remember that you have been sent here for a great and holy work; all we ask of you is to do the best that lies within your power.

After your conditions are more settled, I shall give more minute directions as to what persons you are to hold audiences with, and other matters pertaining to your mission here.

It does not come within my province of action to direct you to the most suitable place, but will throw influences about you to aid you in getting settled. I would like to have you near, or with Col. Daniels and wife. There is great importance attached to your being here, and I shall be happy to give you the philosophy in some of my future papers.

Dr. Rush is of the opinion that you will have no difficulty from the bruise if you are careful, and do not walk much for a few days. Use no poultice upon it, unless it is slippery elm or some cooling remedy. Your Guardian,
Franklin.
Jan. 26, 1867.

My Friend: — The rooms at the corner of F. and Sixth Streets are not the proper ones for you, and the medium has had it demonstrated to him. (This same day the medium had learned that the family was rebel, and had furnished an officer for the rebel army.) I would like to have you, the medium, and Col. Daniels and his good lady, have rooms in the same building, and take board with your friend Mott. Cora was sent here for a great work; her mission here is connected with the medium, and you must all be together as much as you can, as you are all being prepared to work in the same sphere of action.

Be faithful — do the best you can. Each has his part to perform. It is in order for you to meet Senator Howard, as some spirits are desirous of communicating with him upon national affairs. There is no person who can fill your place, or hold the same relation to me. I can give you full satisfaction, but could not give the same to Senator Howard, while other spirits *can* through this source and through Cora. * * * Thaddeus Stevens' Bill does not cover all the ground. (This was a bill for reconstruction.) *More radical and decisive measures must be adopted.* The only way that the South can be fully subdued, is to take all power from their hands. They must be made to feel and realize their errors, before power can be given them to legislate or have any control over national affairs. God will not restore quiet between the North and South, until this is done. *Now is the most favorable opportunity to take decisive measures.* God has summoned all His powers to bring it about. O, man! power will be given you, if you will but obey your highest promptings.

It will be in order for you to write to John C.

Calhoun. Dr. Rush says, " the recovery of your leg depends upon your being quiet. There is danger if you stand upon it too much. No power can protect it if you act in opposition to nature's laws. Keep quiet until Monday, and it will be much better." Your Guardian,
Franklin.

On the 16th of January I was in Boston on my way to Washington. I called to see Miss Barrett, a medium. Soon she was controlled, and a very intelligent spirit announced himself as John C. Calhoun, of South Carolina. I said I could not think it was him, for there was no man in the form or spirit world, whose political opinions I so much disliked. He was a slaveholder, while I was an uncompromising Abolitionist.

He said he had entirely changed his views on that subject, and they were now in perfect harmony with mine, and he would be in Washington with me, and fire many a shot through my battery at slavery.

After being in Washington a few days I addressed a note to him, inquiring if he did speak to me through Miss Barrett, in Boston, and if his views remained as then expressed. Here is his reply :

Jan. 26, 1867.

THOMAS RICHMOND — *Sir :* I have changed my political views. I communicated to you through Miss Barrett. I admire your sterling moral power and practical sense ; you are well adapted to your mission here. Great is your work — spirits will give you thoughts and power to carry out their wishes.

Respecting national affairs, Franklin has more power to communicate to you through this medium than I have, upon national matters. I have not a good control of him.

John C. Calhoun.

In order that Mr. Calhoun's views upon slavery may be more fully established, I copy the following from the *Banner of Light*, it being a communication to his friends upon earth, which came through Mrs. Conant:

May 6, 1867.

"*The Constitution and the Union; or how shall we unite that which civil war has separated?*"

"This is the question that has reached me in my spirit home. Those who knew me on earth, who are dear to me as friends, have earnestly prayed that I would return, giving them advice in this matter.

"It is hardly possible to unite that which is exerting from its center a power to disorganize. The center around which this nation has rallied since that document was formed, is the Constitution, and neither North nor South is willing to give it up, or to sufficiently amend it, as to make it serve the people to-day. How shall we reconstruct? how shall we heal this great, gaping wound? The South utters the cry, the North utters the same cry; and the inner forces that are latent at both North and South, are, it seems to me, already pregnant with the answer.

"It is a fact that souls in individual identity and collectively, are perpetually looking toward the past, to know how to step into the future; and this is right, for men learn by the mistakes they have made, how to conduct themselves in the present.

"To that little group of my friends who have called upon me to answer their question, I have only to say, the same power by which this civil war was inaugurated will reconstruct the Union. Was it the unrest of the South? No. Was it the radical spirit of the North? No. But it was simply the Spirit of the Age, North and South. This same spirit, my friends, will teach you how to reconstruct, and although you receive the light by slow degrees, yet it will come. You shall receive it in its fulness. You will know that your Constitution is not large enough for you. It has shielded you in the past, but in your present proportions you are greater. You have need of something more; and unless the proportions of that document are enlarged so as to make it lose its original identity, it will not answer for you. Your souls are greater and demand greater scope. Parchments never grow, but the thoughts of nations do; and because they do, parchments must be laid aside, and instead of bowing down before them as your guide, your God, turn to the Spirit of the Age, and that Spirit shall teach you how to reconstruct."

WASHINGTON, Jan. 26, 1867.

My Friend: — Visit the House and 'Senate, also the Committee rooms. Suggest and take all means to impress the members with the fact that in order to save the country from a civil war more sanguine than the past rebellion, active measures must be taken. The power must be taken from your Chief Magistrate, and Congress must be prepared for a decisive struggle. More is being done by the President and others who are in sympathy with him to usurp the powers of your government, than you have conception of.

There is much to be done. Congress must show the President that it is prepared, and has the power to control, and will be supported by the people. It is not best to read these communications to any one except such as fully accept and appreciate them.

Go on quietly with your mission, and follow out your impressions. It is not best to refer to spirit communications to persons with whom you talk, but simply make manifest your convictions in a *positive manner!* I desire the greatest good to be accomplished. *Franklin.*

At this time Mr. Farnsworth, the medium, was taken sick, and could not be controlled, and so left Washington for Philadelphia, where his wife was; but he was unable to be used for some three weeks to write, as he remained in an enfeebled condition.

VINELAND, Feb. 7, 1867.

My Friend : — You are doing in Washington all that we require of you, and are an instrument for the nation's good. I think you had better remain there a week or more; your feelings will prompt you when to leave.

Have more confidence, and be controlled more by your impressions. I hoped when the medium was in Washington that his condition would enable me to write through him. There is no way than for him to quit until he regains his health.

I can write messages to you occasionally, without injuring the medium's health.

All will be well if you but look and consider that all things in nature must live out their own lives; no two persons are alike — all have distinct missions, and all have separate relations to each other. You are an instrument in the hands of God, to work out a great good for the nation.

Persevere then, let your highest promptings govern you. High influences will protect and give you support. *Franklin.*

PHILADELPHIA, Feb. 21, 1867.

My Friend : — I wish you to remain in Washington as long as you feel at rest and contented. We are doing with you all that we anticipated, and through you and others are having effect upon Congress. The measures Congress is resorting to, will lead to more radical and decisive action in relation to the South. We hope to carry the nation safely through its present difficulties, without further war. *Franklin.*

VINELAND, Feb. 27, 1867.

My Friend: — It will be best for you to leave Washington on the 12th of March to come here. The medium's condition is such that I cannot promise anything while you are here, but in all probability I can give you interesting papers. I have already accomplished much with you at Washington. You have done well — follow your impressions and feelings. You have become more susceptible and gained much spirit power by going to Washington. Do not allow other influences to disturb your course, but remain firm in your position. Your Guardian,

Franklin.

In accordance with these instructions I left Washington on the morning of the 12th of March, and arrived the same evening at Vineland, N. J., where the medium then was. On the morning of the 13th the following came to me.

March 13, 1867.

My Friend: — You have done well in coming here; you will become acquainted with the place, and visit here again. The medium's health is improving, and he is being prepared to be controlled so as to complete the papers upon the books. Then return to Chicago. You have done well in Washington, but your labors are not completed there. When you arrive at Chicago I will give you more explicit instructions. Persevere — all will be well, and conditions will be so that you will receive all that has been promised.

Franklin.

June 23, 1867.

My Friend: — I want you to be in Washington during the extra session of Congress, and mix with the members as much as possible. Reside again with Mr. Mott's family during your stay; while there, you will receive directions.

When your work is finished at Washington, visit Blue Anchor, N. J. I trust the medium will be so that papers for the books can be given.

Proceed next to Vermont, and visit the parties you feel impressed to. Ever obey your highest promptings. *Franklin.*

In accordance with the above instructions I left for Washington on the 6th of July, stopping a few days on the way with acquaintances, at the oil wells, in Pennsylvania, and arriving there on the 11th of July, at the extra session of Congress. I remained until its adjournment. Mr. Farnsworth being absent from illness, Dr. Franklin used another medium to indicate to me matters he could not impress upon my mind. Congress made a law just at its close, appointing a Peace Commission to treat with the Indians, who were then in a warlike attitude. The Bill named the Commissioners, for the reason that Congress was unwilling to trust the President to appoint them.

I intended Saturday to leave Washington Monday, for Blue Anchor. Saturday evening Dr. Franklin brought a lady medium to my boarding place, and directed me to remain until the Tuesday following, and to visit the President's house on

Monday, and remain until directed to leave. He feared that in President Johnson's ill humor he would veto the Bill. He wished me there to be used as a battery upon him. I did so — went to the White House about 10 A. M., and remained in the ante-room until 3 P. M., when Dr. Franklin said to me that the object was accomplished, and I could leave, which I did. I found the next day the Bill was signed by the President.

Sitting with a medium in Washington on July 16th, whom Dr. Franklin often used to communicate brief messages to me, I remarked that I really wished that I could realize the exact use that was made of me by the spirits. Dr. Franklin wrote through her hand the following: " Channels of communication radiate from you as a center, by which we are enabled to carry impressions to those minds upon which we would operate. Thus it is, you see, that your actual presence is needed.

" I would say to you, be not hasty in the publication of the work entrusted to you. Developments are in progress which will tend to strengthen the array of facts to be presented."

BLUE ANCHOR, July 25, 1867.

My Friend: — Your doings on the road to Washington and while there, are entirely satisfactory, and you have been of great use to the country in going. I did communicate through Miss H., and I desired you to remain over Monday, to see the President. The purpose was served; your influence over the President had its effect. I desire you to go to Boston by steamer. Remain there a few days; visit Mrs. Parmalee, Mrs. Pettie and others, and you will receive communications while there. Make a short stop at Lowell. Visit Daniel Tarbell and other persons in Vermont, and places there and vicinity. Spend about four or five weeks away.

Franklin.

I had no further written messages from Dr. Franklin during 1867. Public matters were progressing, and the public mind developing. Everything of this nature was tending towards a final reconstruction of the government, and a return of the rebel States to their former places in the Union. The President in the meantime was struggling to defeat the salutary laws enacted by Congress for the reconstruction of the States and government, but to little purpose, nearly all power for evil having been taken from him.

CHAPTER XVII.

The winter session of Congress of '67–8, commenced and progressed as usual, not much being done until after the holidays. No call was made for me until the following letter reached me early in February, which I hastened to respond to.

WATERFORD, N. J., Jan. 31, 1868.

My Friend : — It is my pleasure to be enabled to communicate with you; I should have done so ere this, could I have gained control of this medium. I have no directions to give, as the spirit influences about you prompt you to act when necessary. Your powers are still being used in national affairs.

The "circle of three" still continues, and you are becoming developed into a higher condition of thought and action, having increased spiritual capacity to carry out the important mission that is before you.

All your forces are being drilled and organized for effective action. All that is now necessary to prepare your powers to march forward, is to have your spiritual perceptions unfolded, so that you may have *a clear insight of your mission.*

You have already gained a knowledge of the greater share of the work to which you are fitted, yet a clearer spiritual view of *all* the bearings of your mission is requisite, before you can derive the satisfaction you crave. However, you progress as rapidly as the conditions which surround you will admit.

About the middle of February it will be in order for you to visit Washington, and on your way there it may be best for you to remain here (at Waterford, with the medium,) a week or more, in order to get communications. When at Washington you will be directed as to your future course.

Your experience upon the cars was the workings of spirit influence over you; a draft was made upon your brain to affect affairs at Washington.

I hope the books will soon be completed. I have sought some other medium to communicate through, to give the remainder of the papers, but I find none answering the purpose, save him. * * Again I say, let all your mining operations be; you have more important work before you. Prepare yourself for your visit to Washington and other places in order. Your services are required at the capitol. Besides, you will gather much information. Should this letter suggest inquiries, write at once and I will reply.

Franklin.

Dr. Franklin has alluded to an experience of mine in the cars. I was returning from a visit to the country, and about 2 P. M., thirty miles from home, I was suddenly affected as if a ball had been shot from a pistol into my brain. Instantly my head was whirling — I felt dizzy and faint. I imagined I was fatally wounded; perspiration flowed profusely from every pore in my body. I was unable to walk, stand, or scarcely sit, my brain was so wild for a time. I soon began to feel relief, gradually improving until I reached home. I there received magnetic treatment, and by the next day all effects had disappeared. I addressed my spirit guardian to know the cause, and he explained as above.

On arriving at Washington I reported myself to Dr. Franklin by letter addressed to him and mailed to the medium at his residence in Waterford, N. J. The following reply came by mail.

Feb. 28, 1868.

My Friend: — You were inspired to go direct to Washington without stopping here as I had suggested. Your reason must have told you of the importance of going on. I desire you to mingle with the members of the House and Senate as much as you can, so that if possible, I may through your agency, prevent serious troubles to your country.

We hope to prevent bloodshed. Make yourself as comfortable as possible; it would be better for you to stop with Mr. Mott, as I can control his wife better than any other medium in Washington.

It is possible that Mr. Farnsworth may be there before you leave. However, I can answer your letters to me, through him, promptly, and we will hold an active correspondence during your stay there.

It is in order for you to come here after you get through in Washington; then I will direct you as to the places to visit ere your return to Chicago. At present you will give all your attention and strength to Congress. *Franklin.*

March 6, 1868.

My Friend: — I am not interested in the general legislation of Congress. My labor is confined to national justice. The Spirit Congress wish to use you, and have you in Congress when matters that pertain to reconstruction are discussed.

The Spirit Congress were present when the impeachment of the President was presented in the Senate. Washington, Lincoln, myself, and others who had influence with your people or had held high offices while on earth, formed a circle above the heads of the persons in the Senate, you being used as our medium to impart influence to those who were in power, and to impress them to do justice to the people. Your relations to us were nearer than any. We could illume your being, and through you shed light upon others.

Andrew Johnson is doing great service to the country by forcing the radical party to do justice to the negro, yet it is our wish that he be impeached. My object is to have you there nearly all the time of Johnson's trial, so that we may have more influence over the Senate.

I wish you to be in the Senate Chamber as much as possible, and have a comfortable seat. Do not exhaust your physical forces. Keep lively, and be in lively company; concentrate your thoughts upon national matters, but be sure to take time for ample rest.

By observing the above rules, you will be in a far better condition to be used by the Spirit Congress. Your power in the past and at present is great, and will have great influence upon the nation; and the time is not far distant when your people will have knowledge of the important sphere of action you have occupied, and the good you have done your country, by your fidelity to principle and submitting yourself to be used by the powers of the spirit world. It is not in order for me to give coming events. The nation is being severely tried, and more is being done than you are aware of, by the Democrats, to cause bloodshed; still I think we have sufficient power to avert it. Now is the most favorable time to establish right and justice to all.

The radicals will succeed in entirely subduing the enemies of the nation, if they make use of all the means at hand. But the blow *must be quick and decisive* — no time must be lost. The crisis has come; action, action is necessary! My work with you was never needed so much as now. Write me at once. I have more control of you by keeping in spmpathy with you by writing often.

Franklin.

March 8, 1868.

My Friend: — There is great danger that Johnson will not be impeached (by the Senate.) Already the work of bribery has commenced amongst the Senators. * * * There is too much corruption amongst the members of Congress.

Remain in the Senate Chamber all you can; obtain an interview with Senator Howard — he is already fearful of the result of the trial. Tell him that he can use still greater influence, and additional power will be given him from the spirit world. I would not give this warning had I not good reason for it.

However secret Senators or others may be in their corrupt and corrupting actions and doings, there is abundant proof that there are living and intelligent witnesses to every deed, and although concealment may be successful as touching mortals, yet all is made public in the spirit world, and the deceiver will be undeceived when he meets his frauds arrayed against him in spirit life, and must meet a just retribution. "Whatsoever is spoken in the ear, shall be proclaimed upon the housetop."

Take good care of your health. I cannot touch upon any other subject at present.

Franklin.

When I received the last letter, I read it to Mrs. Mott. Dr. Franklin controlled her and corrected an error in it, which I have omitted to copy. Often, between his letters to me through Mr. Farnsworth, Dr. Franklin would control Mrs.

Mott or another lady medium, and give brief orders and suggestions, but he could not give general and detailed directions through them, as he could through Farnsworth.

March 11, 1868.

My Friend: — I had very good control of Mrs. Mott, and I desire you to read all the communications you receive through this medium to her, as it enables me to obtain still better control of her. In order to realize your use, imagine yourself when in the House or Senate, as being like a reflector to a lamp, with small tubes attached, and connected with those tubes wires that extend to and touch such persons in the House as possess sympathetic impressibility. These persons we can influence through your means. I can impress Senator Wade and influence him and many others through you. As the medium was away from home, I could not answer as I desired — and even now he is not in his best condition, consequently I close. *Franklin.*

Before receiving another letter from Dr. Franklin, I received a communication purporting to proceed from highly developed spirits, through the hand of J. M. Spear, inviting me to meet spirit friends in the form and in spirit life, in New York on a given day. I submitted the letter to Dr. Franklin, and he replied as follows:

March 26, 1868

My Friend: — It is not important nor in order for you to visit New York to meet Mr. Spear — the congress of spirits do not desire it.

Your mission at present is in Washington, at the head of the government. There is where we wish to use you most, and where through your instrumentality we can accomplish great good.

Stick to the post until your mission for the present is ended. *Your powers are needed now at Washington, more than at any other time.* The great national struggle is yet to come. Next week will come the trying hour, and it remains to be seen, that those who are now on the side of right will be firm, and combine their forces. Unless they *do*, greater trials are ahead. There is one important communication I have given, that you have not received. It must be in the P. O. in Washington. *Franklin.*

For the past month, and especially for a week or so, my forces had been so drawn upon by spirits in the House and Senate, that I had become quite exhausted, and about 9 in the evening, while chatting with a group of friends, I suddenly received a shock as though a ball was shot into my head. I did not fall, but grew wild and dizzy. My daughter, who was present, took charge of me. This extreme effect gradually gave way, and in a few hours I recovered. The sensation was so strange that I wrote to Dr. Franklin to know the cause, and he replied to me.

March 29, 1868.

My Friend: — The shock you experienced was in part produced by spirit influence upon you, so as to prevent complete exhaustion of your physical system. It was necessary to throw this influence upon you, or you would have been prostrated by sickness. The shock you felt was a favorable symptom, showing that you possessed sufficient vitality to overcome any disease likely to prove serious to you. It is important that you take particular care of yourself now, as you are in a very susceptible condition. While at Washington, stop where it is most convenient, and you can derive most comfort.

By having you in Washington, we have used you as an instrument to accomplish great good to the nation, and can now exert some influence upon Congress, even if you are not present; but if you can remain a while longer without inconveniencing yourself, it will be our pleasure. We believe the crisis is passed; nevertheless, there are obstacles to be conquered. The party in power are not combined, and unless it improves all possible opportunities, serious troubles will be the result. It does not come in order to speak of your mission with Senator Wade; it will be given in due time.

Franklin.

April 6, 1868.

My Friend: — The nation has great dangers to surmount. At Washington there is a set of men combined, whose aim is to assassinate the leading men of the Republican party, and unless great precaution is used by the government, there will be more blood shed in Washington. These men have their victims selected, and are preparing in secret to carry out their hellish designs.

We are using all the influence we can to frustrate the fulfilment of their plans, and to carry the government safely through its present trials. It is best for you to remain in Washington until after the trial of Johnson. Your mission there is of more importance than you are aware of.

Great results will follow. * * * The national troubles that commenced in 1860 are far from being settled; there are yet great difficulties to overcome, before you can have settled peace.

God works in a mysterious way. One of the important and ruling influences that will establish harmony and justice among your people, is spirit influence, which has awakened and manifested its power among you. As conditions become more favorable for good spirits to use the power which God has given them, there will be greater power used by them, and spiritual science will become more general and manifest itself in all the affairs of earth.

You have been selected to operate in governmental, national, and the social affairs of earth, because you were the best fitted to fill the position. Others are selected for other departments — you have been faithful to your mission. You have made great progress, although you may deem it slow — but have patience unto the end, and you will receive full satisfaction.

Franklin.

My prostrated state of health had been such that I wrote to Dr. Benjamin Rush, (spirit,) for advice and prescription. He said I labored under bad cold, congestion of the lungs, and prescribed medicine. He said it would not be safe for me to stay in the Senate Chamber when it was crowded.

April 14, 1868.

My Friend:— Do not exert yourself too far to attend the trial; go only when you feel positive and amply able. Take great care of your physical system, and rest all you can, for since you have been at Washington, you have been greatly drawn from. All your physical resources have been used, also your mental powers, and now you need rest. Wait patiently the result of the trial. There is good cause for doubting that Johnson will be impeached, but we hope to conquer.

. A secret order has its center in New York City, and has organizations all over the land. It is composed of rebels and adventurers, and Democrats give them their aid. Unless active measures are taken to break up this order — suppress it wholly — it will cause a greater war, and more bloodshed than the nation has ever experienced. It is the duty of Congress to take measures at once to crush it out; it has selected all the prominent members of the Republican party for assassination. These members should be protected — they must be made aware of their danger.

Franklin.

[Extract from Letter of April 19, 1868.]

* * * In operating upon other minds, I use yours, and I can have more power over the person I wish to influence, if your thoughts are concentrated upon him. I have less influence on others, when your mind is upon other subjects, or wandering. The place where you board is satisfactory. *Franklin.*

[Extract from Letter of April 26, 1868.]
* * * I fear these great obstacles will not be overcome. There are symptoms of great trouble. Stick to your post; I am with you all the time. I can impress you, and your promptings will be the best guides for you.

Franklin.

Philosophy of Spirit Control.

May 4, 1868.

My Friend: — In communicating with the beings of earth, we are entirely dependent upon the conditions of the medium and his surroundings. There are no two alike — like different musical instruments, they all produce melody, but cannot be played upon in the same manner. There are *special laws* that govern one medium, which cannot be applied to another.

We cannot pursue the same subject through every medium. Any matter which is intricate, or independent of the medium's knowledge, before manifesting, we prepare the medium *specially for ;* we cannot give the same ideas through another, no more readily than you can produce a good growth of corn upon barren soil. Spirit manifestations are as dependent upon proper adaptation, susceptibility, and impressibility of the medium, as corn is on having soil adapted to it, or room to produce growth.

Concerning Mrs. Mott, I have very good control of her, but I have not the same power over her to communicate upon the same subject that I have over this medium. * * * I think this explanation will make the matter clear to your mind — if not, I will explain further.

I said through Mrs. Mott just what I desired, and I use her to advantage. All the forces are required at Washington. There is great danger ahead, but we hope to overcome the enemies of the country. *Right must prevail.* Follow your impressions.   *Franklin.*

[Extract from Letter of May 10, 1868.]

* * * If Johnson is not impeached by the Senate, come at once to the medium's, and I will give you directions. There is much I want you to carry out, for your own benefit and that of others — the good of humanity. I have impressed parties to furnish tickets to the Senate Chamber. When it is necessary for you to be there, the way has been opened, as tickets will be furnished.

Franklin.

'Tis proper to state here that 2,000 tickets to the gallery of the Senate were issued for each day of the trial of Johnson, by the Sergeant-at-Arms, and after supplying the officials, members of the House and the Diplomatic corps, the remainder were distributed amongst the Senators, according to the constituency they represented. Ten tickets were wanted to every one that could be obtained. Each Senator distributed to his friends and constituents as he felt disposed. I had no greater claim upon the Senators than others. None could enter the gallery without a ticket. They were furnished me, as Dr. Franklin promised.

The day before the final vote was taken upon impeachment in the Senate, I wrote the following letter to Senator Trumbull, from our State.

WASHINGTON, May 15, 1868.
HON. LYMAN TRUMBULL —

Dear Sir: Under the peculiar circumstances of the national government, I beg to present to you a few thoughts briefly. To-morrow is the day appointed for decision touching the innocence or guilt of President Johnson — whether he has committed high crimes or misdemeanors in his office. I am glad to feel that you are not publicly committed to vote against *all* the articles of impeachment presented against him, and that you may support some of them.

While I regret that you do not see clearly the propriety of sustaining nearly or all the charges presented by the House of Representatives, I am not vain enough to hope to change your vote upon any one of them; still I shall be better satisfied with myself by expressing a few thoughts to you upon the subject.

It is to be regretted that a few Senators, just at this most important hour of American life, should by their action, not only reverse their own former decisions so frequently made by public vote, but reverse the universal judgment of the great Republican party; for there is scarcely a Republican of intelligence but has already given judgment of impeachment against him. Strange now, that a few Senators are found who had rather impeach themselves, the Senate, and House of Representatives, than to impeach the President.

Who is the President, and why is it such a fearful thing to find him guilty of a high misdemeanor and remove him from an office he has misused and disgraced? Is it any worse for him to be removed from office, than it is for another man — a Stanton? Are not removals of some kind of almost daily occurrence? Why shudder and tremble before this one man, and save him from his just deserts, when by so doing you confront and contemn the judgment of the nation?

If the final vote of the Senate fails to impeach and displace Andy Johnson, who will ever believe that it is the verdict of honest, conscientious judgment? Who that knows Johnson's life, words and acts for the past three years, believes that he is innocent of *all* the charges brought against him? *Can you, can any Senator, vote him innocent of all the charges and specifications brought against him? You must not, you cannot spoil your good Senatorial record by voting that man innocent of all these charges?*

I have been proud of our Senator from Illinois, *whom my vote elected to the Senate some fourteen years ago.* Truly Your Friend,
Tho. Richmond.

On Saturday, May 16th, I sat in the Senate during the session. The vote when taken, was 35 guilty and 19 not guilty; it required one vote more to remove him from the office of President. The Republicans who voted him innocent, from motives more than questionable, were Messrs. Fessenden, Trumbull, Grimes, Henderson, Fowler, Ross, and Wiley. As soon as the vote was announced, Dr. Franklin said to me, "Now, go direct to Waterford, to the medium's house." On the 18th I arrived there, and reported myself to Dr. Franklin, by a note handed to the medium. He replied on the next day.

May 19, 1868

My Friend: — You did well to come here as I desired. I told you to come, and you heard my voice. I fear great troubles yet in Washington, and it is quite probable that it will be necessary for you to return there. If you should, it will be for some weeks. The medium is in good condition. * * * It will be well for you to remain here two or three weeks. I think it best for you to stay here until I know positively you are not needed at Washington. There will be a great storm in national affairs yet to encounter, and there never was a time when I desired your services more. You must perceive the propriety of remaining here, that I may give you immediate instruction

Take all the rest you can. I desire to communicate to you as often as I can, until matters at Washington are more settled. *I wish you to remain here.* *Franklin.*

WATERFORD, May 25, 1868.

My Friend: — The reason I made a change in the winter of 1862–3, by substituting a letter for your going to Washington to see the President, was, that I perceived you could not at that time exert as much influence in an interview as by sending a letter. Your writing had the desired effect. The means used was the influence that we imparted to the President through you. *Had we failed in using you, and in opening the channels through which our influence could be felt in national affairs, the rebels would have succeeded.* The war was brought about to do away with slavery — it could not longer be permitted.

The spirit world had its instruments on both sides, to excite the people. John Brown was the first in the hands of the spirit world to bring about the conflict. At present but one step has been taken and made permanent towards the freedom of the negro and his equal rights.

I fear the most severe conflict is yet to come, before God's commands are faithfully complied with by the American people. You are now gaining much strength and can be used efficiently. It will not be necessary for you to go to Washington at present. You can go to New York in the course of a few days. Go there and remain until you are directed to leave. You will be impressed with regard to these matters, and your judgment will guide you. * * * You will go to Boston and Vermont before you return to Chicago. * * * The medium is too much interested in other matters to be controlled as much as I desire. Should you wish to leave, write to me at once.

Franklin.
May 28, 1868.

My Friend: — I did communicate to you through the medium to whom you have referred, Miss Barrett, of Manchester, N. H., in the summer of 1862. It is not necessary for me to repeat in this letter what has been told you by Dr. Franklin and others concerning your mission, and the influence that is exerted and impressions made upon the administration of your government and all national affairs. I belong to the Spirit Congress, and am conscious of your fidelity to the cause in which you are interested. I know the importance of your relations to Dr. Franklin and the nation, and the power that can be made manifest through you, upon the leading statesmen of your country.

You were selected from the first for this great work by the Spirit Congress, and means have been taken by those who have you in charge, to develop you for the labor, to answer the requirements made by your circle of spirits, as fast as your condition would allow. Step by step you have progressed in this work, and as your power becomes unfolded, new avenues of thought and action are opened to you, and you see more clearly the responsible position you occupy.

You are gathering important papers to be published, but ere the book can be completed, momentous events of a national character, which you will be called to take part in, must accrue. You are being fully armed and equipped for the severe contest which is near at hand. Although there may be much bloodshed it is God's will, and must be obeyed. To purify the nation and remove the obstacles which retard the progress of true development — to make all men free and equal — is the grand result which we are striving to bring about, and you are one of the most reliable instruments we have to aid us.

It is desirable that you mingle with friends, so that your powers may be fully alive, and you can gather all the physical and spiritual strength you can. For a few months to come you will not be located long in one place; you will hold constant communion with Dr. Franklin. Abraham Lincoln will soon communicate to you — he is with you much, but could not communicate to you at the time you wrote him, owing to conditions, which were unfavorable.

You are growing more impressible and can be more easily guided. Continue steadfast to the end, and all will be well.

     Your Friend,   *I. T. Hopper.*

June 13, 1868.

My Friend: — Although I have no important directions to give, I communicate that I may keep in close connection with you. Concerning national affairs, matters are about the same. I am endeavoring to reach Gen. Grant, and surround him with influences that will make him more susceptible to the Spirit Congress. The hopes of the loyal people are centered in him, and he will prove the protector of the American Republic, if his present supporters are persevering and remain true to the good of the nation.

There is much to be done to secure his election, and you will be used to bring it about. That is, an influence will be exerted through you to that end. I wish before that takes place that you would take means to become familiar with him. It would be well for you to correspond with him, setting forth your mission, and suggesting to him that if he will seek and make himself open to spirit influence, that a large circle of persons who have filled the highest offices of the nation, now in spirit life, will aid him in his election, and remain with him during his administration.

Lincoln is not yet prepared to communicate, but will at the proper time, both to you and Gen. Grant. Take special care of your health, as much will be required of you in the course of a few months. *Franklin.*

On receipt of this communication, I wrote to Gen. Grant as requested. I told him that I was received a message from Dr. Franklin, of the above import. This letter opened a magnetic connection between Gen. Grant and myself, which was available to the use of spirits.

[Extract from Letter of Nov. 3, 1868.]

* * * The unanswered letter has not been received. Soon after Congress meets I want you to go to Washington and call here on your way, and take treatment from C.

Franklin.

CHAPTER XVIII.

It may excite remark on the part of the curious, that the spirits with whom I correspond, and the large circle of spirits that surround me, whose names I have incidentally given, were persons of fame and high standing officially and otherwise, when in earth life. Also, that twelve more should be added to my circle, of like standing. I have only to answer that it is an arrangement of the Spirit Congress in its higher wisdom to best accomplish its designs. Nevertheless, as my mission was of a national character, and my powers were to be used upon statesmen, in the control and management of governmental affairs, it would seem perfectly natural that the influence around to inspire me, should be of that character.

Although there was a continual correspondence since June kept up between Dr. Franklin and myself, there was nothing essentially different or interesting upon the war, or reconstruction of our government, until the following communication.

WATERFORD, N. J., Jan. 1, 1869.

My Friend : — The circle of spirits controlling you and the medium are passing through a change.

There are twelve more to be added to your circle, and all will act in full accord with me. During this change I cannot communicate at length, as I have to let go the position I hold in order that the others may act in concert with me. The doubtful letter will be satisfactorily explained. You will be protected during this change, if you follow your impressions and feelings.

You will be needed at Washington soon; at present, remain where you are, until all the conditions are ready for you to go forth. Meanwhile, correspond with me, and I will answer all that is possible. This is from your guardian spirit.

Franklin.

[Extract from Letter of Jan. 6, 1869.]

* * * In arranging a new circle we bring more vigorous influences to affect you and the different mediums we come in contact with. It gives an increase of power to you which is necessary, and comes in order at the present position of our labors. The old circle is retained, new members added. By this addition you will be better enabled to fulfil your mission. *Franklin.*

I arrived on the evening of Jan. 17th at the medium's house, after a tiresome ride from Chicago of nearly a thousand miles. The day following Dr. Franklin gave me the ensuing message.

My Friend: — All the original members of your circle are still with you. Lincoln, Prince Albert, and many others who have recently passed into spirit life, have joined the circle, and we are nearly prepared to act with you.

I think now it will be best for you to start for Washington the first of next week. The object in having you come here is to have you receive magnetic treatment from C. You will also be of great assistance to the medium and his lady; changes are about to be made concerning them, and you can be the means of assisting their controlling spirit in making the best arrangements for them during their stay here. * * * You will perceive the object of your visit here is to prepare you fully for your work in Washington. Write me every day. *Franklin.*

Jan. 24, 1869.

My Friend:—You have made good use of your time here, and are well prepared for your work in Washington.

There is a magnetic connection between you and Gen. Grant. While selecting new officers in government, the Spirit Congress requires you to be in Washington to use you as a medium, that through you, Grant may be influenced to choose proper associates and officers. Hence you will see the necessity for being there, and the importance of your being well prepared for the great work. As matters progress there, you will be informed of your mission and the relations you bear to governmental affairs

I think Mrs. Mott is the best medium for you to consult while there. However, this medium will soon be in condition to answer all required purposes while you remain at Washington.

Franklin.

WASHINGTON, April 12, 1869.

My Friend: — Of late your physical forces have been used by the congress of spirits, and they are not through with you yet. You should read but little, as all your mental powers are required at this time, for high uses. C. is suited to you, and is the instrument we desire. Changes will occur, so that the medium will have the conditions to be controlled to write the remainder of the book. When it is time for you to go to Chicago, you will feel the importance of going. During the summer you will visit New England and other places. Your journey to Chicago is simply to attend to taking testimony in your case, and then you will return here.

Franklin.

April 12, 1869.

My Friend: — It is best that you leave to-morrow morning for Chicago. Get through with your business there, and return here as soon as possible, as you are required here by the Spirit Congress. Your mission here is not completed; your influences are required here for two months to come more than at any time before. We wish through you to work a positive influence upon the Chief Magistrate, and when you return, you will be brought in close contact with him. You will perceive the importance of your mission, and do your best to do as we wish you. I want you to think of Grant, the President, all you can. Think of him when you first wake in the morning; it will assist us in getting an influence over him, to exert for the nation's good.

Franklin.

April 15, 1869.

My Friend : — In using you as an instrument to excite the brain and influence others, we resort to the natural laws of magnetism. We apply the same process of operating upon you as the human magnetizer does upon his subject, the person who holds a negative relation to the operator. When the physical and mental circulations are equalized, you are in good condition, all the organs performing their functions in order, giving a harmonious action of your being. Then the nervauric emanations from your being give us the material to act upon. Each organ of your being produces the quality that it is composed of in the nervauric or spiritual sense; that is to say, *we have an individual, a spirit being, a fac-simile of your being as you now exist to operate upon, in the same manner that the human magnetizer does upon his subject.*

We inspire you to think of some person whom we wish to influence through you — this throws your emanations or spirit in contact and sympathy with him. The action of your spirit is in conjunction with this person, which gives us for the time being control of his thoughts, and we have the power, being positive to you and him, of regulating and shaping those thoughts, and originating in his mental atmosphere new thoughts, aspirations, and resolves. In other words, your mental and physical emanations form a battery, and your thoughts are electrical wires radiating to those we wish to influence. Your thoughts serve as a vehicle by which we send our thoughts; thus you perceive that we act upon the universal laws of electricity and sympathy, to control you, and impress and inspire others, through your nervauric emanations.

When in earth life I learned from experiments the natural laws of material or galvanic electricity, but I did not perceive or comprehend the electrical emanations from the human brain, or electricity so subtile as to escape the senses, yielding chameleon like and susceptible of endless diversities, a condition where the machinery of life is laid open to our gaze — a condition of the brain concentrating a degree of excitement which makes that organ predominate over all others — a condition where the machinery of life lies naked, to be regulated and controlled at will, where a thousand results can be obtained, which no material electricity could effect.

Comparatively few scientific men of your day are willing to fully recognize the fact that the psychological emanations of our minds are capable of affecting those of others, either by contact or proximity — but the phenomena of contagious diseases are so frequent and so indisputable, that no intelligent man ventures to deny them.

Franklin.

April 22, 1869

My Friend: — You are having an influence upon Grant — continue to think of him. If circumstances do not favor your return here at an early date, it may not be important for you to come until autumn.

I shall help you in material matters — have no fears. Give attention to your suit, and as much time to national affairs and Grant, as you can spare. Write often. *Franklin.*

I left Washington as directed on April 13th. I was interested in a very important lawsuit in the U. S. District Court at Chicago. An unexpected notice reached me that testimony would be taken on a given day, and that it was important that I should be there. It was to be present at the taking of this testimony that I returned, supposing that it would require but a few days, when I intended to go back to Washington; but the delay was so great, I did not return then. In June I went to New England by direction, and remained until October, when I returned to Chicago. About the time of my arrival home, the medium, Dr. Farnsworth, arrived at Chicago from California. He had an appointment from the Post-Office department in the summer as mail agent upon the Pacific R. R., which he had filled until he was brought to this city by spirit influence, when through him the following papers were given for this book, in the order in which they bear dates.

During the past summer I have received many

letters from Dr. Franklin on subjects important and interesting, with remarks upon and allusions to the nation, reconstruction, and the government, always pivotal upon the principle of justice. That which I have already published, I deem sufficient to satisfy any intelligent and honest mind that the Spirit Congress, under God, has been engaged in and virtually controlled the measures that have emancipated four millions of slaves, and again brought peace and quiet to the country.

CHAPTER XIX.

As I stated in the last chapter, Dr. Farnsworth came unexpectedly to Chicago, neither of us being aware of the object of his coming, until **Dr.** Franklin revealed to me that the Spirit Congress brought him here to give through him a few closing papers to complete the book upon the war, and also give what papers he could through him, upon social science. Some of the first given were upon the law of control and the conditions necessary to enable the spirits to write those papers through his hand. As they are interesting and instructive, I give them first; they will help the reader to understand how the intelligent spirits are able to communicate to the people of earth.

Oct. 19, 1869.

My Friend: — I am very happy to have the power to give the communications necessary to complete the book; but as I said before, to accomplish my plan in giving these communications, it requires more than ordinary conditions. We have to make *special ones.* It is necessary for you to confine your thoughts as much as possible to the subjects that I am writing upon, while the medium is being controlled to write, and your mind must be free from business cares, and in sympathy with no one but the medium. For the time being give *all* your energies to the work, and so conduct yourself that your mind will be clear and vigorous. The medium is required to pursue the same course. * * * No human being has sufficient individuality and strength to acquire riches, and at the same time use and develop his spiritual faculties.

The means that you resort to in the accumulation of money are antagonistic to spiritual unfoldment. We sometimes have power to assist persons in pecuniary matters, when the use of the money is devoted to spiritual improvement; the controlling influence must be assured of this before any aid can be given.

There is no class of human beings requiring more sympathy and appreciation than well developed mediums. There are times when they require as much protection from the beings of earth as a delicately organized child — they should have guardians in human form to look after their welfare. The condition of society as it now exists amongst you, is antagonistic to spiritual culture. Thus you see the various obstacles that mediums have to overcome, and the opposing influences we have to contend with — but notwithstanding all these, we are gaining ground.

The practice of *rigid economy* does more to unfold the spiritual capacities of mankind than can be derived from associations or societies.

I should never have enjoyed the use of my faculties as I did in earth life, had I not practiced rigid economy. I never could have been a philosopher had I not been an economist. I never could have performed good to my fellow man, had not I been consistent with the laws which governed my being.

Through economy I was taught how to live and enjoy all possible to be enjoyed upon earth. I am now realizing the blessed results of my course, and am delegated by powers above me to communicate to the beings of earth, and you are one of my best instruments.

Franklin.

Oct. 20, 1869.

My Friend: — The use of your powers are of as much consequence to me in giving the papers, as those of the medium. I impress you — the emanations from your being are the positive currents that regulate and hold in place the powers of the medium, so that I may bring my influence to bear upon them, and control them to give my thoughts.

In the first place, if you are in proper condition I impress you; if you receive my impressions and write accordingly, the first condition is fulfilled by you, necessary to receive a communication from me. In reality the matter or thoughts I wish to convey to you are already formed, and if you could then be rendered sufficiently negative, you would be controlled to write the answer to your letter yourself, but you cannot have the two powers operating at the same time — consequently, I bring into use the powers of the second person, (the medium,) still using the positive magnetic influence emanating from your being, upon him, as a motive power to propel and keep the machinery in motion, to telegraph my thoughts to you. When your condition and that of the medium is right, you receive my thoughts clear and unmixed.

Much depends upon your condition when you write to me, as you are the first to be used to excite the train of thought. Study well, look into all these fine conditions, and if there is aught you do not comprehend, write me and I will explain.

Franklin.

Oct. 23, 1869.

My Friend : — In communicating to you by writing, your spiritual emanations and those of the medium, form the instrument for me to control; your emanations are the material necessary to use to enable me to act upon and use the emanations of the medium. Both combined give me the materials to construct the spiritual electrical battery which I use, exactly as I would use a telegraph instrument, to transmit messages. Your mode of telegraphing is visible — you perceive it through the normal senses.

The telegraph I use is invisible, as you can perceive it only through your spiritual sight; you are the first agent used to enable me to produce the communication. The message you receive from me, however, is not colored or in any way influenced by the material you furnish — as my influences are positive to yours, thereby giving me the power to originate and communicate thoughts entirely foreign to your perception.

Every organ of the brain has its spiritual counterpart, which forms the spiritual emanations. The quality or condition of the brain gives off similar qualities and conditions to those of the spirit. Hence the more intellectual and spiritually unfolded and refined you become, the better; you give us a finer quality of material to use to aid us in giving communications. In proportion to your spiritual culture you will receive communications superior to your originating. Although the first condition is taken from you, the communication does not partake of your thoughts, and your mind has no influence whatever upon those I give.

My system of communicating can only be understood by the analysis of the action of electricity in all its component parts and powers.

Your system of telegraphing is the working and science of *material matter*, while mine is the science of *power and life* — and as the controlling agent is above the instrument, spirit above matter, cause above effect, so it can only be appreciated through the spiritual perception of man.

Were the communications you receive a reflection of your mind, I should have no need to use the powers of a second person; you could be controlled to write your own answer. By bringing into use the second person, I gain positive controlling power over your thoughts.

Mind and spirit are one; they are organized electrical substances, taking individual form and action. Spiritual electricity is of the nature of mind, only general in its province of action — permeating the universe, having no limit to its movements. *Franklin.*

Lincoln to Richmond.

CHICAGO, Oct. 24, 1869.

THOMAS RICHMOND — *Sir:* With pleasure I communicate to you. While I was Chief Magistrate and during the war, you wrote to me setting forth the course to be pursued, to enable our armies to be victorious and abolish slavery. Your letter was considered by me, and the plan you suggested was favorably received.

A few of my confidential advisers by whom I was then surrounded, Senator Howard, Stanton, and some members of the House concurred with me in the means you set forth, but I met with great opposition from the leading Generals in the field, and but little support from the result of the councils held upon the matter. God in His wisdom, kept the subject before me, until I was made to stand alone; and the power which I conceived came from God, whom I had recognized and obeyed for many years, commanded me as the only alternative to *put into action your instructions.*

When under the influence of the Higher Power, no human agency could change my purpose.

I obeyed the mandate, believing that through you as an instrument from God, the command was given me.

It proved the deathblow to slavery, and our armies were victorious. I also received other letters from you, which strengthened and supported me in my views. God communicated to me through you and many others. He also influenced me without any apparent instrumentality. I believed as you do in the means He used to make known His wishes to us. It was His power that sustained me through the severe and trying circumstances by which I was surrounded.

I can now perceive that I was *simply an agent or instrument in His hands* to conduct the rebellion in such a manner that slavery might be abolished. I had but few supporters among the advisers who were with me. My support came from God, through the ministration of His instruments. You were used as an instrument to give me strength, and your help came when all other resources failed, and at the most perilous hour of my administration. If you wish to have more from me write and I shall be happy to reply.

A. Lincoln.

Washington to Richmond.

CHICAGO, Oct. 24, 1869.

THOMAS RICHMOND — *Sir:* I am happy to be able to communicate to you. I now see the power that aided and controlled me to establish American independence. I was God's chosen instrument to assist in ushering into existence the great American Republic. In our counsels we foresaw the result that African slavery would have upon the nation eventually, but supposed as it advanced in wisdom, slavery would be abolished by the voice of the people.

Through God's instrumentality all means were used to make the nation comprehend its condition, and the terrible injustice that was being allowed to flourish in its midst, and the necessity of emancipating the negro. His means were of no avail. The people did not comply with His demands, consequently from necessity He caused the rebellion, in order that they might be obeyed.

We sat in council in spirit life, those who had formerly held counsel while at the head of your government. We selected our instruments, fortified them with power from God to go forth and eradicate the great stain upon your government. You were one of our chief instruments to act in a silent manner upon the leaders who deliberated upon the affairs of your nation.

Dr. Franklin, the philosopher, had you in charge and directed you. You have been obedient to his wishes, and faithful to your charge, and the main object of the war has been attained. You have also been used as God's instrument in bringing about the reconstruction of the States.

You, like myself and others whom God chose to perform missions for the good of humanity, will reap a rich reward. You have served our purpose well, and I recognize the good results of your labors. I have counselled you from time to time, and feel pleased that you have kept a record of all that has transpired, and trust that all men will read and believe in God's wisdom and goodness to our fellow creatures.

Washington.
Oct. 26, 1869.

My Friend : — A great and powerful nation sustained and encouraged human slavery — a sin in the eyes of the Ruler of the Universe. The people were being cursed by its effects.

This great sin could be removed only by war and great suffering. The Spirit Congress, composed of those who once held positions on earth, were delegated by the great Ruler of all things to institute conditions through the power that they could exert over human beings, of mingling among the leading men of your land, and selecting the one best fitted to inaugurate a new state of things, and to hold firm to justice, and soar above the selfishness and inhumanity of those already in power, surrounding him. With all the adverse influences that opposed him on every hand at the commencement of his administration, Mr. Lincoln was made strong and wielded a great power over the nation, because he was just and good, and was sustained by the Spirit Congress, they using you as their instrument to approach him, and open the avenues of his being to the illumination of wisdom from the spirit spheres.

At times he faltered at the task before him, as he had none near him who could perceive the great good to his fellow man that he was accomplishing. Even he could not perceive his real mission. God had selected him for the work however, and had provided him with a staff, on which he might lean, when doubt and uncertainty oppressed him.

The struggle commenced — battle after battle was fought. There was no other way to remedy the evil; necessity demanded the slaughter of human beings upon the battlefield — the leading characteristics of the enemy's madness made known, before the nation would awake to the enormous evil that existed in its midst.

We had communicated to Mr. Lincoln through your instrumentality, the course to be pursued. Some Senators assisted him in maintaining the plan we set forth in your message to him — he acted upon it. Then the death-knell of slavery sounded throughout your nation; the manhood of the race then in bondage was recognized by him — they were ordered to stand side by side with the white man on the battlefield, with equal privileges, and free themselves. Thus the abolition of receive wisdom and strength from the higher powers. You were directed to form a circle in Boston, in 1861, of three persons, and the members were told to set for the purpose of establishing magnetic conditions or batteries, you being the chief instrument used to form the conditions.

Through your magnetic relations, or on those electrical cords emanating from your brain, we impressed those persons who sat in council upon the affairs of your nation, during the war. After the war during the sessions of Congress, while the States were being reconstructed, you were sent to Washington, to mingle with the members of Congress, that by your coming in direct contact with them we could exert more power over them, and through your influence have the States reconstructed according to the wish of the Higher Power. The States are now nearly reconstructed, but your labors with Congress are not completed.

Franklin.

CHICAGO, Nov. 5, 1869.

My Friend : — Concerning the impeachment of Johnson, the Spirit Congress was satisfied with his trial. He was impeached in the minds of the American people, and the course pursued throughout his trial, was in accordance with the wisdom from the higher spheres — their object was attained.

The emancipation of the Hebrews from Egyptian bondage was brought about by the same power and instrumentalities from God that produced the emancipation of the negroes from American slavery.

You, Lincoln, and others were used as God's agents, and were controlled by the same magnetic laws that controlled Moses and Aaron to emancipate the Hebrews.

You were being prepared through God's agency for the important part you filled, for nearly forty years. God foresaw and determined what in justice must be accomplished, and prepared His instruments for the work.

Franklin.

I had supposed that the preceding papers covered all that was designed by Dr. Franklin and other spirits for this book.

The medium having arrived at my house, to remain a short time, and the publication of this book being near at hand, I wrote to Dr. Franklin, asking him if he desired to give anything further for it. In reply, the following message came.

CHICAGO, Aug. 13, 1870.

My Friend:—It is with the highest satisfaction that I give you a paper to close your book. The record of the instructions you have received from the spirits who have had you in charge, and your movements and doings during the rebellion — the instrumentalities used — the power exerted over President Lincoln — your mission made known to you — the abolition of slavery brought about, as prophesied by us — all these establish the great truth of spirit communion, and show that you were chosen by God to fill the same mission that Moses did in the abolition of Egyptian slavery.

This great good to humanity has been accomplished, and you now have the satisfaction of witnessing the results. The American nation never was in a more prosperous condition, because the stain of slavery has been removed, and there is more general harmony at the center of your government — more amicable relations between the North and South, and the people generally are more susceptible to the laws of progress and reform in all departments of earth life. They are more susceptible of spiritual culture, because the power that has produced so great a change in your nationality is still with you, working and manifesting itself in all departments, for the highest good of the people.

You have been the instrument in overthrowing a great evil, and you have a greater good to perform in establishing social conditions of a higher order than now exists, before you pass from earth life.

The American people are a favored nation, and have much cause for gratitude. They are susceptible, energetic and persevering; they are more generally susceptible to the subtile and magnetic conditions that favor spirit control, than any other people. This is the reason why what you term Spiritualism has progressed more, and manifested more power among you, than in any other land.

Before the birth of your nation, God foresaw the conditions that could be established to advance Christianity and spiritual culture. He brought his forces to bear upon your nation, and step by step it has progressed, and as fast as the people have been prepared to receive light, it has been given to them.

John Murray, the founder of Universalism in America, was sent from England, a medium, to your shores to proclaim his mission — to do God's service. He was faithful to his charge, and performed a great work for the good of humanity.

To give him more faith and enthusiasm in his labors, God had a church and home erected for him before his arrival, by a man wholly unknown to the world, or Mr. Murray. This man saw the vessel that bore Murray, ere it anchored, and proclaimed to the inhabitants of the town that his minister was on board, and would preach in his church on a given day. He came, and all was brought about as God desired, through Murray, his instrument.

Thus you can trace the progress of the American people, in politics, in religion, in science, the fine arts, and in society — with the same power which controlled you during the rebellion, to bring about the purpose for which you are adapted, and which God designed from the commencement.

This spirit power has operated upon your nation since its birth — but not with the power which it now holds, because the magnetic or spiritual relations of the people were not sufficiently unfolded to furnish the requisite conditions. As soon as the power could be made manifest to the people it was done, and with the most available instruments.

I desire the reader of your book to peruse with care the record of *your doings* connected with the late rebellion, and he will find the manifestations of power entirely outside of your nature and development, completely opposite to the bent of your faculties, showing that a high and unseen influence had you under its control, impelling you to action, and that no power but the Divine could have controlled you to pursue the course you have.

Franklin.

CHAPTER XX.

To the patient reader who has carefully perused the previous pages, I have a few words to add. This book claims the same authority that is claimed for the Bible. So much of it as is not merely personal history, came from the Divine Mind as manifestly as any portion of the Bible.

The modes of life of mankind have greatly changed since Abram pitched his tent in the shadow of the oak on the plains of Mamre, and Sarah, the mother of the Hebrew nation, baked her cakes in the ashes — when the world was young, life was simple, and man was true to his nature.

Something less than four thousand years ago, God raised up a new nation, by calling Abram and Sarah into the wilderness. He made them the parents of that numerous offspring known as the Hebrews.

In process of time these people found themselves slaves in Egypt, downtrodden and oppressed. Being a religious people, they cried unto the Lord for help. God heard their cry, and sent them deliverance.

A trifle less than four hundred years ago, God opened the way for a new nation of people in a wilderness — one that had been hidden and kept from human knowledge for this use, until He inspired Columbus with faith that such a land existed, and a desire to find it. He discovered this Continent, and the American nation was begun.

In process of time this young nation became slaveholding, following the example of the lordly Egyptians. The poor African slave, too, "cried unto the Lord for deliverance."

In 1860 "the fulness of time had come;" God heard their cry, and through public sentiment, political and governmental movements, and the madness of the slaveholder, brought emancipation to four million slaves. The analogy is so great I propose to trace it. In each case God took the part of the slave against the master, and sent messengers to appeal to the moral nature and sense of justice of the slaveholder, which had no further effect than to exasperate him, and in return he imposed still greater burdens upon the poor slave.

Having tried the moral sentiments of the people in vain, he resorted to the passions of the slaveholder. Here he found elements of success — the madness of the slaveholder brought freedom to the slave. Both of these cases of slavery were the fruits of avarice — both were commenced by individuals for private gain — both had existed for more than two hundred years — both had become national in responsibility.

In both cases the responsible parties alike resisted all appeals in behalf of the oppressed. In each case God had prepared instruments to work out His purposes, men to act on men, mind to act on mind, and in each case freed the slaves, to the despoiling of the slaveholder. The same God who emancipated the Hebrews wrought deliverance to the African. The same Power that summoned Moses from the sheepcote, called me from commercial pursuits, and Lincoln from the bar. The same power and law which instructed and guided Moses in his work, directed and guided us in ours.

The angel who talked to Moses from the fiery bush, and Franklin, who talked and wrote to me, both communicated through the same power and law, both had the same authority, and were animated by the same grand purpose, justice to oppressed humanity. Moses and myself regarded the call from the Lord alike.

That communication from the angel in the burning bush to Moses, was what is now called Spiritualism. All the passages in the Bible, where the " Lord spake unto Moses," and all other messages, whether through prophet or apostle, coming from the invisible world, are what is termed Spiritualism. Prophets and apostles were what are now called mediums. God has not changed — principles are the same, justice and truth the same, as when God heard the cry of the Hebrews. The methods and intelligence of the people have changed — names and manifestations have greatly changed. All this is Spiritualism now. The modes of communicating are explained in this book; science dispels wonder. What is Spiritualism? I answer, First, belief in man's immortality; Second, a belief that the spirits of men gone into spirit life, *can* and *do* communicate to mortals, by the aid of the natural faculties of both, and *this* is the full sum of its faith. Beyond this there is no central faith; each believes as he is led by evidences. What is the faith of Christianity? I answer, First, belief in the immortality of man; Second, a belief that the departed spirits of men *have* communicated to mortals. The grand difference lies between the words *have* and *do*. The testimony in this book proves that they *do;* the testimony of the Bible proves that they *have* communicated in the past.

For further proof that spirits *do* communicate, I offer the thousands of living mediums and the millions of Spiritualists who are mingling with the unbelievers every day, as witnesses. For proof that they *have* communicated, I offer the sixty-six messages in the Bible called "Books," and the whole array of prophets and apostles — especially the prophet Daniel, chap. 10: John, in Revelations chap. 22, v. 8, 9: Peter, James and John, who saw and heard Moses and Elias talking with Christ, and hundreds of other instances in the Bible.

I quote the Bible as divine authority, not intending by comparison any disrespect for it, but to show that God lives amongst us and has opened up a NEW DISPENSATION to man. Religionists seem to think that God retired from the world nearly two thousand years ago, and left it to grope in darkness. Spiritualists generally believe that God is near us, with us, guiding and controlling the affairs of men, nations, and the universe, He imparting influence and truths to those who believe and will receive them. Every inspired word in the Bible was given through mediums called prophets or apostles in those days — some of it in trance, some in visions, impressions, and dreams. Many of the clergy and opposers of Spiritualism, admit that evil spirits do communicate with mortals, but deny that high and elevated ones do. A minister some years since was appointed by his fellows to examine Spiritualism, and report, which he did, to the above effect.

I doubt not his, or their honesty, in their tests and experiments; this, doubtless, was their experience. The law of attraction governs spirit movements — like attracts like. Seeking fraud and deception, they attracted similar spirits, responding to their expectations.

Christ says, " he that doeth *my will shall know* of my doctrine." Failing to do it, leaves one in darkness, and they cannot discover the truth.

What evidences are there of the truths of the communications through the prophets and apostles, outside of their own assertions? I answer none at all, different from that of mediums now. All the old prophets are self-announced, giving their names and their communications; they give no outside testimony or proof of the truth of their messages. The mediums give abundant tests to living people, and proofs from the spirit world.

If a spirit of "the appearance of a man" could come and converse with Daniel, the prophet; if the spirits of Moses and Elias could return and talk with Christ, so that Peter, James and John saw and heard; if the spirit of one of the old prophets could show John all that he tells in the Book of the Revelations; if a spirit could send Ananias to talk with Paul, and restore his sight; if Cornelius saw a spirit, which told him to send for Peter, and thousands of like cases recorded in the Bible; why may not spirits talk and write through mediums now as well as then? If an angel could talk to Moses, may not one talk to me under like conditions?

I ask, has God changed? Has He repealed the law by which He and spirits communicated with men, in ancient days?

I know that there are those who repudiate this doctrine of spirit communion and manifestations. I know that the church and religionists repudiate the faith and claims of Spiritualism, as the *priesthood and Jewish Church did the teachings of Christ and the Apostles, eighteen hundred years ago*, and repeat "Away with it!" "Away with it!" we don't believe a word of it! To all such I reply, in Paul's language:

"What if some do not believe? Shall their unbelief make the truth of God of none effect? God forbid. Let God be true, and every man a liar."

I ask no one to doubt the truth of the Bible, but I say that *prophets and apostles were men*, and of like passions with men and mediums of these days, and no more likely to be pure and incorruptible, than people of the present age. Inspiration is the same now that it was when Jeremiah mourned over Israel.

www.ingramcontent.com/pod-product-compliance
Lightning Source LLC
Chambersburg PA
CBHW032223230426
43666CB00033B/934